2015 Chokoloskee Island, Fla.

[signature]

Published in the United States of America

By

GBP

Grizzly Bookz Publishing

A Not-For-Profit Organization

All proceeds from the sale of books by Rick Magers are donated to the following.

The Smallwood Trading Post in Chokoloskee, Florida.

Katia Solomon, the girl in Ladybug and the Dragon.

Homeless animal caregivers, wherever we find them.

DEDICATION

To the courageous freedom fighters
wherever they are on this
marvelous Blue
Planet.

Books by this author: January 2012

- Dark Caribbean
- The McKannahs
- The McKannahs ~ together again ~
- The Face Painter
- The Black Widowmaker
- Satan's Dark Angels
- America
- It's A Dog's Life
- 80 Stories
- Ladybug and the Dragon
- A Sacred Vow

All books by this author are available on his website or by contacting him by email. His books and over 100 short stories are available on his Irish pal's eBook website in Limerick Ireland.

www.grizzlybookz.net

magersrick@yahoo.com

theebooksale.com

Printed in the United States of America by Snowfall Press.

A description of each book is on the last page.

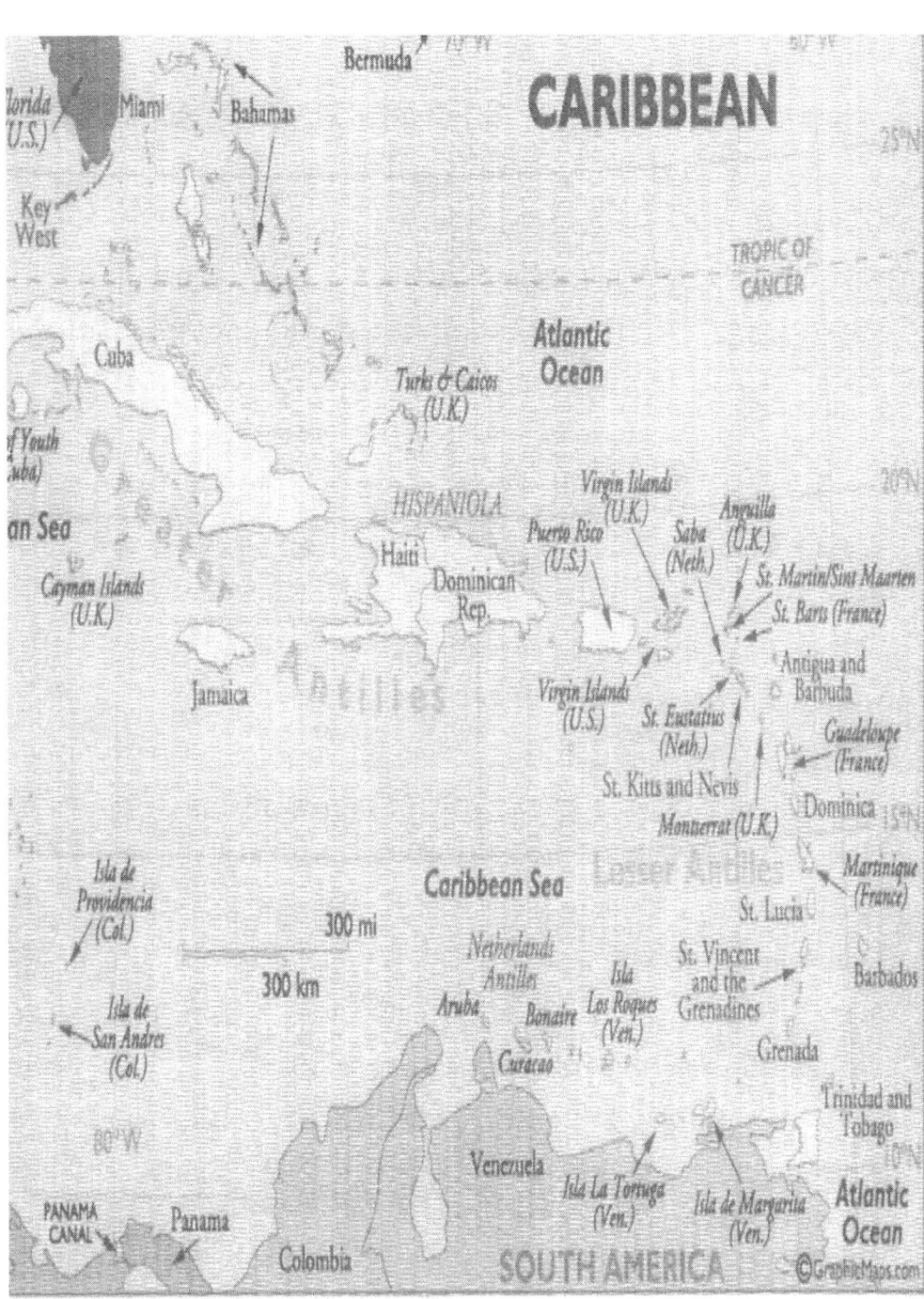

FOREWARD

APACHE—Now, long after they have been imprisoned on squalid chunks of useless land, that word still brings to mind vivid images of terror. Although none of the invading pale-skinned immigrants that experienced the dread of seeing those magnificent warriors coming toward them, as they traveled across their southwest land, are still alive, the word still carries an impact like few others.

One word that does however, to those who are familiar with it, is CARIB. After reading this novel, I believe the reader will forever after associate the word CARIB, as they do APACHE, with a fierce—strong-willed—independent people who were capable of making those who entered their domain wish they had taken a different route.

I have sat in the jungle and listened, as my interpreter passed words from several native storytellers' lips to my ears, about the ferocity of the Carib Indians. Their willingness to battle any and all invaders and his willingness to devour his fellow man sent a chill up my spine. Those traits left his signature as a warning during his time, and it will be the vehicle for their legend's perpetuity.

Today, in the 21st century, throughout the Caribbean Sea and Central America and along the Caribbean coast of South America, children are still frightened when told, "Be good or I will let the Carib cannibals come and get you."

PREFACE

In the year 1493 the explorer, Christopher Columbus, anchored his ship off the Caribbean Island—Guadeloupe. He and a group of his men approached the beach in a longboat.

Sheltered by palms and dense brush, frightened eyes of Carib Indians watched. Strange men with light skin had been there before, and all knew of their treachery.

"They wear clothes that our weapons will not penetrate, and they carry sticks that can kill us from the next village. The thin shiny war clubs they use can easily slice our heads off and they ride giant beasts with heads bigger than the crocodiles, with teeth so big they can bite us in half."

The natives remained hidden and watched as the strange looking men entered their camp.

"Captain, look at this." Columbus walked to the huge pepper pot simmering on a smoldering fire. He gasped when his lieutenant used two nearby sticks that were fastened together to serve as a tool for extracting the ingredients from the pot. A human hand and forearm rested on the sticks with flesh sagging into the stew.

From that day forth, the word CANNIBAL was unjustifiably associated with most of the Indians who inhabited the islands in the Caribbean Sea and the coastal jungles of South America.

Many different tribes inhabited those coastal areas and the outer islands, but most were small peaceful bands that occupied their days with the task of providing food and shelter for their families and themselves. Over a span of centuries many of these small groups merged, providing strength and security against invading enemies, and also as a trading base among their own kind.

One of these groups eventually became the Arawak Indians. Although they had enemies, and would fight fiercely to protect themselves, they were basically a peaceful people. They eventually became strong enough to migrate north as they populated many of the small Caribbean islands and the Bahamas. Perhaps it was their willingness to get along with their neighbors, and also the invaders from Europe, which led to their demise. With little resistance they allowed the invading white men to lead them into slavery—and eventual extinction.

Another group that was formed by merging with smaller tribes was the Carib Indian—a fiercely independent warrior tribe. As their power-base grew, so did the natural tendency to wage war on neighboring tribes to expand their territory. The reason that these two large groups became enemies has been lost within their cultural progress—but enemies they were. There remains today a small group of direct descendants of Carib Indians in an area of Dominica—and nowhere else. They are merely a group of strong resourceful people who understood the necessity of adapting to changing times—to await their inevitable extinction.

Powerful new enemies arrived from distant lands on ships larger than any the natives had ever seen. These foreign invaders would regularly attack the two indigenous tribes and decimate their numbers drastically, but still the Carib fought them and the Arawak at every meeting. Had the two tribes of Indians joined forces to battle the invading Spanish, Portuguese, English, French, Dutch and other Europeans, they might very well have altered history, and still exist in numbers today.

Inbred hatred between the Caribs and the Arawaks kept them fighting amongst themselves as the invaders watched, waited, and then eventually attacked. When the time was right, these strange new men wearing tin clothes, and mounted on huge beasts, while carrying weapons that the Indians had never dreamed of, moved ahead with plans to dominate everything within and beyond their eyesight—which they did and still do today in many areas.

Soon, the Arawak and Carib Indians fell to the harvesting scythe of progress. A handful of Carib descendants, still alive in the 21st century, keep their ancient traditions and history alive by word-of-mouth. The invaders defeated the Arawak, but failed to conquer the Carib. However, they were scattered throughout the Caribbean Sea by the winds of time, leaving only that one small tribe. They too will one day be only photos in the galleries of men, whose greedy ancestors annihilated them.

...

Early in the 16th century, an old Carib warrior-teacher named Atupi gathered a group of young boys to listen as he told the story about two powerful men of these two tribes—opposing enemies of legendary stature. His story has been handed down many times by new warriors like those gathered around as he talks.

He will pass on the story of these two great men. One was from his own people—Ahameke. He was a Carib warrior of great cunning, who believed that only fierce warriors went on to the hereafter where they would live forever and be tended by hordes of nubile women. It was this mighty warrior who created guerrilla war tactics that sent shivers of terror along the spines of seasoned soldiers, and caused dreams to be filled with nightmares—one was cannibalism.

The other was Baracoraima, an Arawak warrior. He was a giant man who stood six-feet-ten-inches tall and weighed two-hundred-and-fifty pounds. He was also a very wise leader who immediately understood that to oppose the invaders was futile. He tried to negotiate with them for supplies to battle his enemy, the Carib, "Who," he told them, "will also become your enemy." He could never have understood the treachery in the hearts of these new men, who had no understanding of honor, and would become a worse enemy than his people had ever known.

Encounters that the Indians of the Caribbean Sea had with the Spaniards and other Europeans during the twenty years after the arrival of Christopher Columbus was the most traumatic they had experienced since their beginning as a race of people, many centuries earlier.

The English, Dutch, French, Portuguese and others soon followed the Spaniards. A lucrative bounty awaited nations that sent their ships in search of spices, slaves, and the one priceless item that all were seeking—LAND. Each nation sent pioneers to colonize the islands. The Arawak Indians were facing two hundred years of misery as slaves, and eventual extinction. The Carib Indians did little better, but they managed to hold the invaders of their land at arm's length until they secured a foothold in areas where the Europeans had not yet settled.

Not long after Christopher Columbus arrived, many of the Arawak Indians were either dead, enslaved, or scattered—never to regroup as a people. With far superior numbers at the time of the arriving invaders, it remains a mystery why they did not fight harder for their freedom? It appears that they went willingly into enslavement.

During this same period, the Carib Indians fought the invaders at every turn, but due to many tragic events, the Caribs also lost their identity as a people. They willingly bred with escaped African slaves, who became known as Maroons. [Cimaroons] They hoped it would increase their numbers, and allow them to carry such fierce battles to the invaders that they would leave their land. But the many sicknesses that arrived with the invading Europeans killed their people quicker than they could multiply, and more efficiently than all of the weapons combined.

To their credit, a very small group of Carib Indians fought fiercely, refusing enslavement and chose to remain distant from the European invaders. Their reward will be eventual extinction—in the near future.

. . .

The people in this story first appeared many centuries ago, perhaps thousands? Scholars and archeologists are still undecided about the date when Neanderthals began branching into other variations of early man. Ancestors of the extinct Arawak, and now nearly extinct Carib, began their initial struggle to survive as a separate species somewhere on what eventually became known as Asia. For reasons, which might remain forever unknown, various tribes banded together for safety and began migrating to *greener pastures.*

It could be explained by a look at animal behavior. Most animals have senses that we are yet to fully understand, and even today will often alert us to danger, if we take time to listen, watch, and understand them—these people did. They didn't question why large herds of animals, which they relied on for food, began a migration across Asia to Alaska via the Bering Land Bridge—they simply followed them. During the next few thousand years many changes occurred in these nomad's lives, as they walked south along the coast of what would become Western North America.

Now in a land where snow was not an ever-present element to deal with, the skin shielding their eyes from the bright white glare began widening—to allow in more light. As all animals have always done, they bred with the indigenous people they met along the way, most of which had been subjected to a greater amount of sunlight, and were covered with darker skin. Now we have males about five feet tall being followed by females about four feet tall. Although the skin surrounding their eyes has opened somewhat, they still retain their original oriental slant: albeit less distinct. They're both much browner now than their kin, who refused to leave the frozen wastelands of Asia to accompany them as they searched for a better life. Those too will eventually follow to create the people who inhabit Alaska today, but the forerunners of the Carib and Arawak Indians sensed a warmer land ahead waiting for them, and did not stop their migration until they reached the eastern slopes of the Andes. From there they began moving down toward the Amazon River and its tributaries, north into the Orinoco Valley, along the green coast of Venezuela to Eastern Colombia, and Guyana, and finally out into the Caribbean Sea to inhabit many of the islands.

. . .

Come with me now and listen as the old Carib warrior Atupi, tells the story of the Arawak and Carib Indians. They will battle each other, and separately wage war with a new enemy more powerful than all of the tribes in their world.

AUTHOR NOTE: Go to page 195 and read the LEGEND INDEX to identify the many gods and goddesses that these people believed in.

1

~ Teaching the legend ~

"**Ahameke was a very young boy when the men who** wear tin clothes came to the land that was our home." Atupi, the old Carib warrior, was now a storyteller keeping his people's history alive. Atupi paused as he looked at each of the five young boys. On this 16th century night, Atupi sat with five young Carib boys high in the dense mountains of Dominica Island, which lies in crystal clear azure water like a priceless jewel in the crown of a king. Their island home is in the central Lesser Antilles on the eastern end of the Caribbean Sea. The boys are about to begin a long journey into the past of their ancestors. The five Carib Indians were all between eleven and twelve years old. Each night after eating their sparse meal, often little more than a few small sweet potatoes and cassava bread, they built up the fire exactly as their teacher had instructed them during their first gathering. For three months they would remain on the mountain gathered around the fire as the legendary old Carib warrior brought the history of their people alive.

"Ahameke," Atupi continued, "had just become a Carib warrior when the terrible men with hair on their faces and wearing shiny clothes, came to his village. He grabbed the hand of Aketoni and led her away from the terrible evil men, and then hid her so he could return to his village."

"Aieee! Aieee! Run fast, Ahameke." It was all that the young boy heard his mother yell, but it was enough to save his life. All had heard about the strange men in shiny clothes that were invading their land. The village cacique—<u>semi-divine chief</u>—sent warriors to spy on the invaders, but when they returned, their information was ignored. It was more than he could believe.

"Men in shiny clothing who ride beasts with many legs are coming?"

The cacique stared hard at his scouts. "You saw this when your eyes were open, and not when you were asleep dreaming?"

"Yes! We all saw them," each of the three young scouts answered with enthusiasm, "and they are coming in great numbers."

This information, vital to their survival, which was ignored by the cacique was a fatal blow to most of the people in Ahameke's village. Of two-hundred, only twenty escaped. The rest were killed that night or enslaved.

. . .

Captain José Areena was a skilled military tactician. Earlier, his scouts had located Ahameke's village and returned with the valuable information he required. The captain was a very thin man who stood a foot taller than the tallest soldier under his command, and he immensely enjoyed looking down at everyone who approached him. At the lowest point of his thin chiseled face was a black goatee. It had the effect of emphasizing the cruel emotionless face above it. The pointed beard concealed a barely discernable, incestuously tiny chin. A set of odd misaligned black eyes sat much too close together atop a crooked pointed nose hanging there like the beak of a buzzard for the entire world to see—cruelty burning hot within deep sockets beneath bushy black manicured eyebrows.

He summoned his officers to brief them, and also to be certain that each understood where to deploy the troops they were in charge of. "We have allowed far too many natives to escape during the last two encounters." His cold black eyes passed briefly by each of his lieutenant's eyes, stopping momentarily to intensely stare...letting each of them know that they had better listen carefully. "We have the opportunity to redeem ourselves in the eyes of Colonel Hernandez. I want a large body count of warriors and a long line of female slaves when we return to the fort. On the next dark moon, which is in three days, we will attack the village that our scouts recently discovered. Our silent, stealthy approach will ensure a great success." He further instructed his ninety soldiers, "We will leave our horses one kilometer from the village with our animal tenders, and then remove all armor before moving forward."

Captain José Areena looked directly into the dark eyes of a short young lieutenant. "Lieutenant Pinosa, you will take fifteen men and move around to the south side of their village to prevent the natives from escaping on a narrow trail spotted by the scouts. One of the scouts will accompany you to point it out." Without waiting for an answer the captain then turned to another young lieutenant. "Lieutenant Camargo, you will do likewise on the north side of the savage's camp." He turned briefly from one to the other, "Do you both understand what your objective is during this raid?" After each man responded with a brisk 'yessir' he continued. "I will be in command of ninety seasoned war veterans which I have personally chosen for this particular mission, and we will strike so swiftly that you may not see many trying to escape, but be alert, never-the-less."

Three nights later, a sleeping Indian village was awakened beneath a pitch-black sky as strangers rushed in and began killing any and all warriors as they sleepily rolled out of their hammocks.

"Aieee! Aieee! Run fast Ahameke, run. Ahhggg, oooh, oooh." Her slender brown hands clutched the razor sharp sword as it entered her stomach. "Aieeeeee!" Her fingers fell, as the blade came out—to be shoved into the belly of the small girl running toward her screaming mother.

Small brown men ran from their sleeping quarters and

frantically attempted to use their weapons. Ironwood clubs with shark teeth imbedded in them were raised high, only to be knocked away by a steel mace as other soldier's blades drew blood.

"Aieee! Ahhggg! Oooooh! Aieee!" A screaming Atupi grabbed his frail body and gyrated around the fire to add emphasis. Swords flashed in the meager campfire light. Sixty soldiers slashed, as thirty perimeter guards prevented most from escaping. Soon after entering the Indian camp, the soldiers were finishing off the dying men, as terrified women and children huddled beneath threatening swords raised high above the heads of strange men with hair on their face.

"Hold on to your children, but you must lie down now." Arawak guides screamed at the Indian women in their own language. "Lay down now or they will kill all of you." The Spanish soldiers remained silent and watched the captives, as their Arawak guides threw wood on the fire.

The blazing fire soon lit a scene of ghastly carnage.

Young Ahameke showed great courage in returning to see if some of his family had somehow survived. None had, but his act of great bravery would be carried from mouth to ear until all had heard the story. He was suddenly, and without training, thrust into the position of warrior. Legends were quickly built around the young Indian who would soon become the youngest cacique in Carib history.

The casual attitude, with which the old cacique had treated the information that his scouts returned with, would never again be repeated. Other Indian villages throughout the area surrounding Guyana would hear about the slaughter and enslavement of the people in Ahameke's village. "We must begin preparations today for our escape from these evil invaders." Indians along the coast of Venezuela and elsewhere began preparing to move into the Caribbean Sea and away from the crazy white men they had been hearing about. One group of those early voyagers, who gathered to paddle their small dugout pirogues into the dark frightening waters which lie north of a land they had considered their home for many centuries, would become known by all as simply—Caribs.

. . .

Soon, other more peaceful tribes would follow, and banded together to be known as Arawak. They settled on the islands on Grenada and St. Lucia. In time, most would move to the island of Trinidad, near the mainland of South America.

Until ships, larger than any that the natives had even dreamed of, brought men in numbers greater than their imagination could conceive, the Caribs left their mark on the history of the islands they tried to settle on and be left alone to live their simple lives in peace. No sooner had they settled on a small island, than the Spaniards and others pursued them. The Carib Indians finally understood that the invaders of their land intended to kill every last one of them.

. . .

Ahameke called a war council with the other caciques inhabiting the nearby islands. Although very young to be the chief of a large tribe of Indians, his courage in battle was already known throughout the Antilles. When all of the caciques were seated around his campfire drinking cassava beer, eating roast iguana, boiled corn, and sweet potatoes, he stood to speak. "The men who wear shiny clothes came on our land with no fear, intending to kill all who did not flee fast enough. We will soon be so few in numbers that there will be no hope of defeating these evil men. We must do something to make them fear us and stay far away from where we live." He stood looking down at the men as they all nodded their agreement. "Instruct all of your warriors that from this day on we will cook the flesh of all white men we catch. We shall eat some to acquire the power of his soul, and leave the rest for his people to see. When they know that we will prevent them from ever going on to the land of dreams, by eating their heart and other parts that they will need to get there, they will stay away from this island and anywhere else where we build our villages."

A small fleet of long, ocean-going, Carib Indian dugouts was soon heading north from Saint Vincent Island, toward Martinique. Both islands sat peacefully in the Antilles, lying north off the coast of Venezuela.

. . .

"When the invaders first struck," their teacher, Atupi, continued, "Ahameke grabbed the hand of Aketoni, who was still a child herself, and only slightly younger than Ahameke. He led her away from the terrible men and hid her, so that he could return to their village and try to save Aketoni's mother. She was already dead, so he returned, and together they fled into the dense forest and hid. Aketoni later gave him three sons: Bapatou—Bababa—Raouti, and a daughter that they named Bameeta. Ahameke treated Aketoni with great respect, and even though he took other females for a wife, so that he could increase the numbers of his village, he let all of them know that Aketoni would always be his number one wife.

Aketoni would often take the hand of Ahameke and lead him to the hammock. It did not matter what he was doing or who he was talking to, he would always smile and walk away with her. They lay in the hammock for many hours making love—her way of maintaining power over the other wives. When Ahameke went to the hammock with his other wives, it was always for only a short time, and then he returned to Aketoni's hammock."

The old warrior/teacher stood and walked around the campfire. The boys all thought he was walking to collect his thoughts, and be ready to resume his stories. Actually, the old man was suffering from severe arthritis, as did many of the older island people due to the constant moisture surrounding them. When the blood once again flowed through his painful joints, and the aching lessened, he sat on his rounded, up-ended log across the fire from his students.

While he was walking out the stiffness in his old joints, the boys gathered fresh soft grasses to cover his seat, and he took time to get settled into them before continuing.

"When Ahameke was only thirteen years old he was already a powerful Carib warrior who was respected by all of his people—young and old alike." The old teacher/warrior stood and raised his arms above his head, even then barely reaching to six feet at his fingertips. The mesmerized young boys leaned forward as he spoke.

"He stood taller than this, and was as heavy as two men." Atupi very slowly lowered his arms as he turned his dark eyes to each student. "He was a giant among our people. I will tell you now of the battle at sea, when the Arawak cacique named Baracoraima was left for dead by our war party." Atupi moved slowly, his thick naked buttocks revolving on the fresh grass, as he turned to face each boy directly...all the while speaking in a low and mysteriously ominous tone. "This giant Arawak warrior, Baracoraima, was also larger than two men, and medicine men today say he is still spying on us because he cannot be killed by mortal men."

Each boy had heard bits of the story as they sat in the dark, while their elders talked and bragged of Carib feats, and their feasting on the victims to leave the mark of terror for all to see. They now waited breathlessly for Atupi to resume the story about the Arawak Cacique that could not be killed except by a God. The old man was a master storyteller who dearly loved his task, often pausing to build suspense. When he finally spoke, it was with a low growling voice.

"He killed all of our warriors." Atupi had been slowly lowering his body until he was squatting across the fire, facing his five students. "Eeeeiieeeeeya," he screamed as his powerful old legs propelled him into the air, waving his wooden, steel-hard, ironwood war-club. Two boys were quite startled and fell backward, but scrambled quickly back to their place on the sitting log as he continued. "Baracoraima was only stunned, and soon came back to his senses. He grabbed his war-club and killed all of the men of our war party. He even killed Ahameke's son Bapatou." The old storyteller's voice was low and came from a place deep within, like the warning growl of a lion. "Remember this story so that you can tell your children of Ahameke's revenge."

. . .

Ahameke's first son, Bapatou, was accepted as the leader of a small group of eight Carib warriors. They departed Martinique Island two weeks before Baracoraima and his band of Arawak wives departed Trinidad. Bapatou and his eight men successfully raided three small Arawak villages during their ten-day run south along the Windward Islands. Men lay dead—all with missing body parts that had been devoured by the victors. Raped women wept for their loved ones, as the Caribs passed them from warrior to warrior. Bapatou was making a reputation for himself and hoped that it would some day surpass his legendary father's.

"We leave for the big land in the morning, but tonight we feast on one of these Arawak pigs." Bapatou smiled as he walked toward the two terrified ten-year-old boys. They had taken them from a tiny island village two days earlier, before moving toward Grenada, an Arawak stronghold where they were now camped in a desolate palmetto-filled, uninhabited area on the southern tip. The palm-fiber rope tied across each boy's mouth suppressed their screams to grunts, but bulging eyes revealed their terror as they moved from Bapatou to the grinning young Carib warriors sitting around the glowing coals. Each strained at the fiber rope attaching arms to feet behind their back. Their terror-filled eyes left Bapatou as they watched the heavy war club being raised. One instinctively closed his eyes as it came crashing down on his skull—over and over. The other boy quivered with fright as he watched.

Bapatou only had to nod his head toward two of his

young warriors. They leaped to their feet and grabbed the body to place it on the hot coals. The two boys were only slightly older than the boy they carried to the fire. "We will allow the other boy to watch us devour his friend, so he can tell his people that to defy the Carib nation is to invite a horror to enter their lives such as they have never seen." The Carib leader, Bapatou, who was speaking, had not yet reached his fifteenth birthday—he never would be.

. . .

At the exact moment that Bapatou was leaving his small camp on Grenada, a large Portuguese slave ship carrying five-hundred Africans went aground on the south tip of Grenada Island. In smooth calm water and mild weather, the captain missed the passage between Trinidad and Grenada. It was a wide channel and deep enough for larger vessels, but he and a drunken crew managed to locate the shallows a short distance from Point Salinese, and tear part of their vessel's bottom out.

Several of the slaves had worked tirelessly since the day they were thrown on the vessel; their common goal was to understand how to release the long steel rods that ran through their chains. When the ship went aground, they immediately removed the rod and began freeing everyone. The captive Africans all got ashore, and when the drunken Portuguese crew of the slaver arrived later, the Africans killed them all. On the continent of Africa they were a notoriously war-like tribe known as Mocos.

The Moco eventually merged with the Carib, but soon became so strong that a special decree was issued by the highest ranking Carib Cacique, to all Carib settlements—*Kill all male babies born to the Moco, but spare the females for our men to breed with.* This eventually caused the Mocos to flee to the mountains and align with the other Maroons, their black brothers who had already settled there. The Carib Indians were never able to rout them out, and from this time on, the Black Carib Maroons grew much stronger as the original Carib Indians weakened, and eventually dwindled to a very small band.

The above-mentioned circumstances eventually split the two groups, but for a short period of time they banded together and waged a terrifying war on all who would deprive their combined people of freedom.

...

"We must go to the fort on the island of Margarita and trade with the strange little men who wear shiny clothes, for their special hard tools." Baracoraima looked at the group of young wives, which he had selected from his many. They were to be used for trading stock, and also to help paddle his dugout canoe across the treacherous channel between his village on Trinidad and the tip of Venezuela. "You are all strong wives and I am certain that you can help take us across Dragon's Mouth Channel, and to the fort of the Spaniards. If the warriors in shiny clothes will accept you in exchange for the tools I need to build a war fleet, then our other people will be safe from the Carib cannibals."

Baracoraima was a huge man that both men and women of his Arawak tribe respected. He stood now and looked down at the men. "You must be alert during my absence." He slowly turned full circle as he looked directly at each man. "When I return with the tools, we will be able to construct this many war canoes in the same time it now takes to make one." He held his huge hands out toward them as he again turned full circle—with all ten digits spread wide to emphasize the importance of his mission.

Pointing toward the sleek thirty-foot-long dugout canoe resting on the bank at the edge of the water, he spoke to the fifteen wives who would accompany him. "When the canoe is filled with supplies and water, put the new hammocks that you are working on with the others, and then tie them securely. If we capsize they will remain in the canoe until we get the water bailed out, and we are inside again. Check all of the calabash scoops to be sure they are strong. Each of you must have one paddle to use when we depart, and also tie two spares inside." Baracoraima looked sternly at each wife—even the older ones who had been with him for many years. "Check your paddles well, because they will be all that will save our lives if we meet the Carib cannibals." When he stretched to his full height, he was an imposing six-foot ten-inch tall Arawak Indian Cacique—an impressive figure to all—especially the small Spaniards who had met him. He waved a powerfully muscled arm, "Go now and prepare, because we leave when the sun arrives."

. . .

As Baracoraima was speaking to his people, Bapatou spoke to his warriors. "We will soon reach the rocks called Los Testigos, and then the big island is less than a day away." He had listened carefully to his father and the others who had made this same journey. He was comfortable traveling across the ocean at night, as they had been doing since leaving their bone and cadaver-strewn camp four days earlier. "We will raid many Arawak camps and take slaves to paddle their own canoes back to our island." His cruel leering face could not be seen, but his men heard the confidence in his voice, and trusted his judgment. "We will be greeted as courageous warriors and will be given the still beating hearts of the young boys as the celebration feast is being prepared to honor each of us." Every young warrior paddled efficiently, a habit developed since they were old enough to hold a paddle. Each dreamed of one day being hailed as a great Carib warrior.

. . .

"Do not lean out when you put your paddle back in the water," Baracoraima scolded his new wife. "Huami," he yelled to his oldest wife, who sat directly in front of Bukuru, "did you anger almighty Emanjah—<u>River goddess: teacher of children</u>—as you were teaching Bukuru how to paddle?"

"She paddled well in the river—this is not a river."

Baracoraima reached between his feet searching the half-gourd for the correct size. When he located it, a yelp of pain came from Huami. "Ow!"

She said no more but thought, *some day old man I will tie gourds full of those rocks around your neck and roll your body into the river.*

All thought him a wizard, but Baracoraima was simply a person who studied everyone, so that he would know how they would act or think. "If you do that, old toothless one, who will chew your meat? Ha-ha-ha, now be quiet and paddle." He searched the gourd bucket for the next lime-size stone, which he would use to keep his wives thinking about their task. "That is better paddling now Bukuru—I will reward you in my hammock tonight." His eyes ran across the twelve-year-old girl's back. *The soldiers will surely want that one,* he thought. *I will trade her for many tools made from the shiny hard material they call steel, which the hair-faced men make their hats from.*

Baracoraima's thirty-foot-long dugout was being pushed through the deadly, unpredictable waters of the passage between Trinidad and Peninsula de Paria, which protrudes from Venezuela's eastern tip. Its reputation is justifiable, because it's one of the Caribbean's most dangerous ten-mile trips. "All of you pull together now, you lazy women, or mighty Yayjaba—<u>Creator of the world</u>—will send you to Yemaya—<u>Goddess of the deep sea</u>—who will let Ghede—<u>God of death</u>—hold you in her arms tonight and love you."

He threw a stone and hit the front paddler in the back of the head, proving again that his accuracy with the simple weapon was not legend but fact. "Do not drag your paddle, silly little woman. Push the water behind you then reach forward swiftly for another paddleful."

He alone of the sixteen occupants in the slender vessel understood the potential danger they faced during the brief voyage to the mainland. Baracoraima used a short steering paddle to keep them on course, but his dark eyes were constantly searching the horizon ahead and to each side for any sign of an approaching enemy.

It is too calm, the weather & ocean-wise sixty-year-old Trinidadian Arawak Cacique thought. *This would be a good day for a Carib war party to be out on the water.* "Rhythm," he yelled as he bounced another stone from a young wife's head. "Get in rhythm, all of you sorry women, or we will sleep in the water tonight, and ever after." His concern would soon be justified.

. . .

"Pull hard my lusty warriors," Bapatou yelled, encouraging his young Carib warriors to paddle harder. The previous night, as he was asleep in the stern, he suddenly came wide-awake. A dream vision caused him to alter his course toward the island of Trinidad.

He had quickly awakened the other sleepers to tell all of them about his dream. "Guabancex—<u>Goddess of the ocean storms</u>—this night, only moments ago, sent Guantuava—<u>Guabancex' messenger</u>—to my dream-self. We will now go to a land called Trinidad, which my father spoke of many times. On the way we will meet an Arawak with many women, then kill him and take all of his women home with us."

Bapatou also paddled, but he continuously scanned the skies. His young mind recalled stories of sea voyages that he had been told since a child. Using his well-developed memory, he positioned each group of stars in his mind during the night, just as they had been related to him. By maintaining his course during the night, when the sun rose from the sea once again, he was able to set the same course by observing the cloud formations and the direction the water was moving.

During the night, his dark eyes scanned the stars until he was certain he knew what course the canoe was on. "Turn slowly left until I tell you to continue ahead." His men did not say a word as they began pulling harder on the starboard paddles to bring the bow to a position slightly east of south. "Now go straight."

After the youthful warriors had corrected the course, they were heading straight toward the Dragon's Mouth—and Baracoraima's dugout canoe full of women.

. . .

Each of the five boys on top of the mountain remained silent as they listened to Atupi weave his story about the past adventures of their ancestors. Their thoughts followed a similar pattern, as did all of those boys who had come to the mountain with Atupi in years past...*I too will be a great warrior, so my people will tell stories about my bravery. I will kill many Arawak and take their women to be my slaves.* Each young boy also watched the glowing coals of the fire he helped maintain. They all knew a lot about the three months they would spend with Atupi, even though it was forbidden to speak about the time spent with the old warrior. However, a word here and a word there always spread through the village by the last group to come down from the mountain. One dark ominous thought constantly worked its way through each boy's mind. *I wonder which one of us he will choose for the supreme test on the final day?* A tremor of fear ran down each boy's spine as that thought passed through, even though they knew nothing about the final test. It was one aspect of a young warriors training that he never spoke of if he survived it—on threat of death.

. . .

With the eastern sun on his back, each half-hour Bapatou stood and spread his toes over the gunwale to scan the calm ocean ahead. Before the sun had washed the darkness from the sky, he spoke. "Paddle gently, so I can see what is on the edge where the water falls from our world." His eyes had detected a spot that would have gone unseen by most. "Move the bow to the right a little and pull hard on your paddles." He stood often to determine if the spot was a low flying sea bird, a rolling dolphin, or a canoe traveling between a small nearby island and the big island called Venezuela. "Ahameke has told me many times that Arawak men go to the big island to trade with the little men who wear shiny clothes." He stood again. "**Yes**," he screamed, "it is a canoe traveling alone. Pull hard and we will send them all to Ghede after we take what we want."

Baracoraima also had the eyes of an eagle, and spotted the vessel to his right only a short time after it turned toward his dugout. He watched but a moment to be certain they were altering course to intercept him. He quickly calculated that he and his wives were over half way across Dragon's Mouth Channel, so it was better that they continue and hope to touch land where other Arawak villages could offer assistance. "Carib war canoe," was all he said—all he needed to say.

The older women knew the meaning of those words from their own experiences, or stories told by those who had survived Carib attacks. They began leaning into their paddles as though their very lives depended on their own strength and ability—it did.

Baracoraima knew that his female paddlers could never outrun a Carib war party—not even the three miles remaining to reach the mainland. He began paddling as he kept his eyes on the other vessel. *Yes,* he thought, *I was correct, it is the Carib cannibals, but so far I see no other boats.* He strained to see ahead while thinking, *it is an ambush and their other warriors will cut off our escape with more canoes.* "**Pull**...**pull**...**pull**," he screamed, "I see only one dugout. Paddle with all of your strength and we might get to land before they catch us."

The old warrior had been in many battles on the ocean, but had never seen one lone Carib dugout canoe attacking. He leaned into his short steering paddle, but kept glancing toward the attackers. *They are gaining,* he thought. He soon spotted land dead ahead and yelled encouragement. He knew that outrunning the small, swift, war canoe was a futile attempt, but he encouraged his wives, so that their vessel would be as close to land as possible. "We can get to land before they catch us if you push the water behind you as if you do not wish to be invited to their dinner tonight. Pull the water...push it behind, pull...push." The yelling was robbing him of his strength, so he concentrated on his own paddle.

A thousand yards from land he felt certain that the

Caribs would be in his dugout in moments.

They were!

Bapatou's dugout raced alongside and all nine young men jumped inside Baracoraima's larger vessel. All of the Carib warriors were very young and inexperienced, but all had listened to their village elders; men who had been in many battles at sea. They expertly used the frightened screaming women as shields, so that the old Arawak warrior they were facing in such close quarters could not get to them.

"**Eaters of people**," Baracoraima screamed loudly as he swung his ironwood club—tiger shark teeth imbedded in both edges. "Baby rapers—fuckers of dogs—eaters of shit—children with tiny pissers." He screamed insults in hopes of distracting them, and throwing their timing off. *Help us, Ogoun*—God of war—was the last thing he thought before Bapatou lunged with his war-club and landed a blow against the old Arawak's head. He went unconscious as Bapatou hit him twice more on the back of his head. The old man lay face down in the stern.

"Sit still now or we will kill all of you." Bapatou felt a rush of confidence, knowing that he would be known as the Carib who killed the legendary Arawak warrior. He stood near Baracoraima's *dead* body and issued orders to his female captives. "You! Old one, stand." Huami, who was brought because Baracoraima knew she could help control the young wives, stood immediately and barely grunted as the ironwood war-club hit her from behind, knocking the toothless old wife of Baracoraima overboard. She splashed about in a daze until one of the other Carib warriors hit her in the face twice with his war club. Bukuru watched as she sank beneath the surface.

"Stand," he belligerently ordered another of the older women. Bapatou slowly moved forward as he inspected the women cowering in the boat. He glared at thirty-four-year-old Amatinu as she slowly rose, but in a flash of movement she was overboard and swimming beneath the surface away from the dugout as fast as she could. "Look, look." Bapatou laughed, "The old hag is going to catch a tiger shark." He stood laughing as she surfaced and continued swimming.

His toughest warrior already had one of Baracoraima's young wives bent over the gunwale and had entered her from behind. Each man prepared to do the same as Bapatou stood guard. "Ha, ha, ha, look." He pointed, "Rataguana is on his third one. Hurry or he will have his seed in them all, and every child will be ugly like him. Ha, ha, ha. He wants his own tribe of ugly Caribs." The women remained silent and prayed to their god Loa—<u>Protector of humans</u>.

The Carib warriors were enjoying moving from woman to woman in the two canoes, now tied together and stable. Baracoraima was finally regaining consciousness but lay motionless in his own blood as he used his hearing to construct what was happening behind him. His huge old fingers still instinctively gripped his war-club as he watched the shadow of a man standing nearby. Still he did not move so much as an eye muscle. He knew the man would be watching the women being raped, so he finally moved his head enough to observe the scene through eyes opened barely a slit. *This child is their cacique*, he thought, *and if I can kill him then the others will be weakened because they are all very young.*

Baracoraima said a silent prayer to Loa as his fingers tightly gripped his war-club as he readied himself. The first sound made was the tiger shark teeth on his stout club entering Bapatou's skull...*thawack*, knocking the young Carib unconscious and overboard. The other eight warriors were at a terrible disadvantage as he stormed toward them. All had been in such a rush to enter the women that they only lowered their belted breechcloths instead of removing them—a fatal mistake. Two were beaten to death while still inside the women, and catapulted from the dugout. In moments two more were brained and tossed overboard. The other four made desperate attempts to grab their war-clubs and do battle with the giant, which they now believed was a war-spirit-come-back-from-death.

The women saw certain defeat turning into victory—one that would be told for centuries around Arawak camps. They held tightly to the enemy's war-clubs and began biting, scratching, clawing and head-butting the legs of the Caribs. Baracoraima bludgeoned two more and threw the bodies into the water. The remaining two yelled and jumped overboard to escape the man who would live in legend as: The Arawak Warrior Who Will Not Die.

Looking around the canoe, Baracoraima asked where Huami and Amatinu were. "Huami is dead," Bukuru said, "she was killed and thrown in the water, as Amatinu jumped into the sea. I watched Huami sink after her head was busted open."

"**Quickly**," Baracoraima yelled, "we must untie their dugout and find old Amatinu. Butubi, keep your eyes on Amatinu if you see her." The entire battle lasted only a few minutes from the moment the Caribs entered the Arawak dugout. His wives were scrambling to quickly untie the Carib dugout. "Butubi, get in the small canoe with Dashumi and follow me."

He didn't hesitate a moment, and pointed to his new young wife, Bukuru. "Get in with Butubi and Dashumi and do as they say." The twelve-year-old girl leaped into the Carib dugout and grabbed a paddle. "We must find Amatinu if she is alive."

Sixteen-year-old Ashatani said quietly in a quavering voice, "The Carib cannibal's killed Huami with a war club, but Amatinu dove in the sea and swam away too fast"

Baracoraima picked up a discarded paddle, and with his remaining wives, began looking for Amatinu. "Stop paddling," he said, "stand and look across the water for her." They were still close enough to hear the screams of the two Carib warriors who had jumped overboard.

"Look," one of the women said, pointing toward the screaming young men, "sharks are eating the eaters-of-people. Yee, yee, yee, wooeee" she screeched. "Do they taste good?"

"**Yee, yee, yee**," they all yelled loudly. One of the older wives yelled, "Do not bother with their little pee sticks because they are very small." All laughed as the two young men were being torn apart only yards away.

"Paddle," Baracoraima commanded, "they will soon be shark shit, and we must find old Amatinu before the sharks do." He balanced himself on the gunwale with his toes spread to grip the wood as he steadied himself with his steering paddle. He motioned with a wave, and Bukuru, Butubi, and Dashumi moved out in the Carib canoe and began heading toward the area he motioned toward with his free arm. He noticed that all three of his wives in the canoe began paddling harder.

"**Yeeiiyeee!**"

He turned to see Butubi yelling and waving her paddle as she pointed ahead of her dugout. He could see old Amatinu waving back. Baracoraima's two boats were soon alongside.

"It is a nice day for a swim, old woman," he smiled at her as she prepared to re-enter his dugout canoe. "Did you enjoy yourself?" The old warrior would die without revealing that she had always been his favorite wife because she would not be told what to do—ever.

She looked him straight in the eye as she held the gunwale and tread water, saying with no expression at all, "When my cacique takes a nap during a fierce battle, then I must swim to find a better man."

"Fierce battle," he grumbled, "I was only scolding those Carib children."

"If that is how you scold them, then please leave mine alone." He turned toward thirteen year old Dashumi who was speaking, and just shook his head.

"To have good young wives a man must keep them away from the old ones who talk too much." He motioned toward the Carib dugout with his blood caked head. "Four of you get in with them and we will continue to the fort and do our business."

Before anyone had time to move, Amatinu said, "Clean your bloody head old warrior or the little white men will believe you too are a savage like the Carib cannibals.

. . .

When Atupi paused in the telling of his story about the giant Arawak Cacique, one young soon-to-be warrior asked with eyes wide, "Could Baracoraima really not be killed?"

The old man paused and looked intently into the boy's eyes. At some point, this same question was always asked by one of his students. Storytellers like Atupi often took the stories about one of the strong caciques, and changed him into a ghost-like—god-like legend. He now lowered his voice to a whisper so that the boys were forced to lean toward him. "When he left this world, he went first to the mountain where Ghede waited. Ghede said that he was not only the God of Death, but that he was also the God of Ghost Warriors." Atupi paused and looked from one boy to the next.

"There," Atupi said so quietly that the boys all had to lean farther toward him. The old man nodded very slightly with his head toward a point behind them, and spoke a little louder, "There." All of the boys were now straining to hear his words. Atupi spoke louder as his foot pressed the leather bellows that he had years earlier stolen from the Spanish. "Baracoraima is there in the distance watching you."

When the boys all turned to see what he was staring at, Atupi pressed harder on the bellows hidden beneath the leaves. It forced enough air through the clay tubes, fitted together and buried beneath the fire, until it picked up smoke through the pipe stems in the tubes and pumped it out the buried end, twenty feet away.

"Aieeeeeeeeeee," each screamed, as the ancient Arawak warrior materialized in the misty distance—in their young minds.

When Atupi stopped pumping the bellows with his foot and the spirit-vision of the legendary old Arawak Cacique disappeared. "Aieee...aieeee...aieeee" came from every mouth as the boys stared wide-eyed into the misty night.

The old magician said quietly, "he has moved back into the night, but he will always be watching you. Come, build the fire and I will tell you what the iron men did to him and how he made them pay for their treachery."

· · ·

It was not yet noon when the two dugout canoes reached the tip of Peninsula de Paria and began skirting the coastline of Venezuela toward Isla de Margarita. It was almost one hundred and fifty miles away, so they stopped on the coast each night. Baracoraima was well known for his size and bravery, but after this voyage and the stories his wives told, he would become a legend in his time and ever after.

2

~ Arawak Giant ~

Baracoraima guided his dugouts to the Arawak villages that he was familiar with. Each afternoon, during the five-day trip along the Venezuelan coast to the tip of Peninsula de Araya, he repeatedly sought out familiar landmarks. His destination lay on the tip of the isthmus protruding toward Isla de Margarita.

"Hola old warrior, come and sit at my fire." Each village cacique greeted the huge old warrior similarly, as his two dugouts made their way west. "Have you killed many Carib cannibals since you were last here?"

"He killed twice this many yesterday." Amatinu held both hands out with the fingers spread wide.

Baracoraima grunted as he waved her away. "She always sees ten pigs when there is but one then wonders why I only brought home a single pig for our dinner." He turned and watched her walk toward the women's fire. "I should have given her to the sharks long ago."

Baracoraima learned very young that he did not have to boast. Due to his enormous size, compared to the others of his race, who seldom stood much taller than five feet, others had carried many tales of Baracoraima's feats far and wide, and his reputation grew as he aged.

"Come with me old friend," the village cacique said to him, "we will drink cassava beer and feast on a tapir that we killed four days ago."

"Yes! I love the meat of tapir, old friend." He smiled at the village chief as he rubbed his stomach. "I have not tasted it for many passings of the round moon."

The cacique was proud to be able to offer the legendary warrior a food that he enjoyed. "It has been hanging from a tree with spices and fruits that my old woman stuffed its belly with."

"Ahhh, I can hardly wait." Baracoraima rubbed his still tightly muscled belly again. "Your old woman always puts good spices in the tapir to make the flavor better."

"My young wives will also make cassava bread and sweet potatoes with fresh honey to honor a visit from the mighty Cacique Baracoraima."

As they walked toward the fire pit where the tapir was slowly roasting, a young man came to them with two calabash cups filled with pungent cassava beer. He handed both to his cacique before returning to his spot at the smoldering fire. Tapir was a treat, and all enjoyed watching it roast. "Here mighty one," the old cacique said, handing one of the cups to Baracoraima. "Drink and relax. When you leave we will pray to Olokum—<u>God of the ocean depths</u>—and ask that he not call you to come live in his home, and also that he lets you complete your journey to the island where the men in shiny clothes live in a big house surrounded by trees that never grow leaves. A trip such as that can be very perilous."

"Yes," Baracoraima answered after draining the cup, then holding it out for a refill from the same young man. "Olokum has always been good to me, so we too will pray, because I am not ready to visit his house yet."

The local cacique accepted a refill but asked for a large gourd full of beer to be brought to each of them. "Now old warrior, tell me about the many men you killed yesterday."

"They were only children and very few."

. . .

"Captain!" A thin young private with a red pointed beard called, "Come and see what is coming toward us in the canal." He stood, nervously pulling at the tip of his goatee beard until his commanding officer, Captain Christopher de Cordova Bolivar was thoroughly brushed by his barber. While buttoning his jacket, the captain looked at his image in the full-length dressing mirror. He did not see the image on it, preferring instead the one that he had created in his mind. The pale face he saw was not a small child-like face with perpetually oozing pimples, and the murky eyes of a hyena...but rather a strong handsome face with powerful black eyes that radiated wisdom and authority. He turned away from the imposter, and like a feisty bantam rooster, the captain strutted ahead of his private toward the ladder leading to the observation tower.

After observing Baracoraima through his long telescope he turned to hear the young soldier say, "Very strange that the large dugout is Arawak and the small one is Carib, but there appears to be only one man with many women."

Before raising the glass again the captain said, "Get one of the Arawak up here to interpret for me." He stood on his tiptoes, intently studying the huge man as the young private scrambled down the ladder.

"Hola, Baracoraima." After hailing the old chief, and then listening to what he said, the Arawak turned back to the Captain. He spoke in near perfect Spanish, a language that he had learned in the three years he spent working for the

Spaniards. "It is the mighty giant, Cacique Baracoraima, and he wants to come in and do business."

"Tell him he is welcome to put his canoes on land. He has my permission to bring his women and wares into the fort." Captain Bolivar put the glass back to his eye as the diminutive young Indian communicated his message to Baracoraima. While in his special, custom-made elevated boots, the Spanish captain stood only slightly taller than the Arawak Indian who was climbing back down the ladder to greet the giant—he never left his quarters without them on his tiny feet.

Baracoraima was legendary among the Arawak people, and was already being mentioned frequently among the Spaniards in the area. The captain had difficulty holding the long heavy telescope, so he rested it on the edge of the tree trunk wall, while remaining on his toes so he could see through it. "My God," he said aloud when Baracoraima stepped from the dugout, and stood nearby as his wives pulled his canoe, and also the Carib prize, up on the bank beside the river. *A man that large is very dangerous*, he thought as he watched through the glass. After a few more moments of observing the huge Arawak Indian, Captain Bolivar said to himself, *I will use him to show these ignorant savages how much power I have over their lives.*

Baracoraima was completely unaware that his size had placed him in jeopardy with the complex little professional soldier. The inept Spanish captain was in complete control of every living person and animal that entered the fort.

"Bring all of the hammocks," Baracoraima instructed his wives, "even the ones we have used. We must trade everything we can spare if we are to get the tools to build our war fleet. We will sleep on the ground during the trip home." He watched as his wives loaded the bundles of hammocks on their heads.

All of his women wore nothing above their small skirt, and some not even that, as they followed him toward the huge gate. Word spread as the naked and nearly naked women worked outside the fort. Soldiers now lined the narrow ramp running completely around the inside of the fort's pole walls. The ramp was over five feet below the top of the wall, with shooting holes cut out, so that they could fire their muskets without exposing themselves. The sex-starved soldiers crowded together, with some at the shooting holes, others on their toes, and the rest on boxes watching—wishing—daydreaming.

The fort was not without women, but the officers and higher-ranking enlisted men had purchased all that were young and attractive. Their caciques who came regularly from Venezuela to barter were happy to acquire the objects that the Spaniards offered, and more women could easily be had. The lower ranking soldiers had only the older, lumpy women to barter with for bed favors. They watched the honey-colored young women moving around just below the fort walls, and in their lusty imagination spent pleasurable moments with the young girls, especially those with small firm breasts, which quivered alluringly as they walked.

The captain scampered down the ladder and rushed to his quarters, calling to his two Arawak servants as soon as he entered. Two old men came running from the clothes they were washing for their master. They were happy to have a job that allowed them a meal each evening, and a room inside to sleep on the floor. "Get my dress uniform with all of the medals on the jacket." The bent old man started to follow his friend, but Captain Bolivar stopped him with a loud command. "**Boots**! Azuba, get my dress boots with the extra high heels, and if they are not shiny then shine them first"

An hour later he stepped majestically out onto his porch looking like the commander of a glorious fleet of Spanish ships. In fact, more powerful men saw smallness in every aspect of the little man, and had abandoned him to the jungles of a small island. His soldiers were all picked from men who were of no value to Spain—except to hold the frontier until qualified men could take their place. Their lives were meaningless to the Spanish Crown. Powerful men in

Spain often commented, "We trade useless men for extremely valuable property, which is a truly marvelous bargain."

All of his men detested the little captain, but obeyed his commands, fearing possible future reprisals. Many had seen men such as Captain Bolivar rise to lofty positions of great power. Lieutenant Alfonso quickly straightened to attention when his captain called his name. "Yessir."

"Where is that giant cannibal who came here with only women?"

"He's not a cannibal sir, he's an Arawak Cacique from Trinidad."

The diminutive Captain Bolivar turned to stare at his second-in-command. "I did not ask for an evaluation of the man." His words were clipped and sharp, "I asked you for his whereabouts."

"Very sorry sir, he is with the men in the canteen, and all of his women are waiting over there." He pointed to the group sitting beneath a mahogany tree.

"Carry on Lieutenant." Captain Bolivar stepped from the porch and walked stiffly toward the enlisted men's canteen.

Lieutenant Alfonso glared at the man, *that little rooster walks like he has a canoe paddle shoved up his ass.* He turned back to his sergeant's young Arawak woman. "So Umelli, are you going to come to my bed after Ramiro goes on watch?"

. . .

Captain Bolivar stepped into the room, and momentarily stood against the log wall, next to the door opening. After his eyes were adjusted to the darkness of the room, he spoke quietly to one of his men, "Corporal Sancho."

"Yessir," the young man sat his pewter beer mug down on the small table in front of them, and leaned toward his commander, "what can I do for you, sir?"

"Locate Lieutenant Alfonso quickly, and tell him to have ten armed guards in full uniform with him when he reports to me in my office within the hour." He stared hard at the young soldier a moment before continuing. "Then you come to my office and wait outside until I call you." Without waiting for a reply, Captain Bolivar spun about, exited the canteen, and strutted stiffly across the compound toward his single-room office, which sat in one of the fort's log buildings.

Once inside, Captain Bolivar walked up the three steps to the area where his desk was positioned, then sat in a chair that was also on a raised platform. His knee length boots, with special elevated heels and soles, barely touched the floor. He enjoyed looking down at all whom he had summoned. "Enter," he said loudly after the knocking stopped. His face was a mask of emotionless authority as he looked down at the Lieutenant.

"Have your men standing at attention on each side of the door. After Corporal Sancho leaves I will explain to you what I want done." He then yelled for the young man waiting outside with the soldiers. When Corporal Sancho was standing at the desk looking up at his commander, he was given his orders.

"Tell that cannibal savage that I want him here in my office immediately."

After the door closed behind Corporal Sancho, Captain Bolivar looked down at his lieutenant and spoke softly, but the cruel eyes within his stone-like mask burned fiercely. "This is what you are to inform your men."

Lieutenant Alfonso listened with disgust, but saluted smartly and spun about when he was dismissed. His thoughts were vile as he closed the door behind him. *It was my worst day when I was sent to serve with that little fool. I fear it will eventually cost me my life.*

Baracoraima listened to the very young Arawak servant as he interpreted the brief message that Corporal Sancho was delivering. The giant turned to the mixed group of Spanish civilians, servants, and off-duty soldiers—all of whom had learned the Arawak language. They had been drinking cassava beer and Spanish wine, while intently listening to Baracoraima's lusty stories about his entourage of young wives. He was on a mission, and wanted to get the most he could for his merchandise, so he embellished every detail. "Your chief has asked that I come to him." He drained his beer from the pewter mug, and then admired the utensil made from a material he had never seen. "I would like to have one of these when I return to my camp."

As he followed the corporal, he thought, *the stories that I have heard about these people are not true; they are a pleasant tribe.* He glanced at the many buildings within the huge fort, but slowed as they passed the blacksmith's shop. He had no idea what the man was doing as he pounded on the dozens of hoops for wooden barrels, but instinctively knew that it had something to do with the tools he was here to negotiate for. *These are people who can help me rid this land of the Carib cannibals.*

Baracoraima had to stoop as he entered Captain Bolivar's tiny log office building, which further humiliated the inept, diminutive Spaniard. Baracoraima was looking intently at the tiny man seated behind a beautifully carved mahogany box, and didn't notice the ten soldiers enter with him. When he stopped at the wooden railing, which served to prevent anyone from entering the desk area until invited, he was looking straight into the small soldier's dark black—now infuriated eyes.

Captain Bolivar had never seen a man as huge as the savage in front of him, but had ten good reasons not to be intimidated. His ten reasons had quietly formed a half-moon behind Baracoraima. He spoke to his Arawak interpreter, but never removed his eyes from Baracoraima. "Ask him what gifts he has brought his great Spanish conqueror?"

Baracoraima never took his eyes from Captain Bolivar, as the young Arawak native interpreted. Baracoraima's dark unblinking stare further enraged the little commandant.

Baracoraima descended from a people who had survived in a hostile land for centuries prior to the emergence of Spain as a nation. In his world, every chief was equal in courage and wisdom until proven otherwise. It was unacceptable to cower to another chief—regardless the size of his village.

Shrewdness in all dealings was respected the most, as the mark of a powerful and potential ally. He responded as though he was dealing with an honorable chief. "I have brought no gifts, but I have many hammocks to make your nights more comfortable and lovely women to make your dreams more pleasant. In exchange for these items I wish to return with some of your hard tools, so I can construct a war fleet to destroy the Carib cannibals." He paused a moment as he looked deeply into eyes that he now felt were without emotion, and cared about nothing at all—beyond his own pleasures. "If I can rid the world of the Carib, then it will be a better place for you, me and all who follow us into this world."

This was his first encounter with the representatives of Spain. He was about to learn what all others before him had learned—they were not an honorable people. They viewed all others as merely enemies to be defeated, or chattel to be used as they saw fit. Captain Bolivar contained his fury toward the giant standing before him, who conversed as though he was speaking to an equal. *That savage did not even have the courtesy to bow before speaking to his conqueror. That is inexcusable.* He spoke in a very calm, moderated voice. "You come before your new master with no gifts, and refuse to bow, and then expect me to deal with you?"

The captain's quivering voice betrayed his frustration when he leaned slightly toward Baracoraima. "What are we to do? Build a fire in the center of my fort and eat one of my servants as we discuss your needs?" He waited until the interpreter had finished, and then nodded his head toward Lieutenant Alfonso.

Before Baracoraima had time to fully comprehend what had been said, a musket butt hit the back of head. Two others hit him as he fell. "Tie him securely," Captain Bolivar said, "and put him in the strongest cell." He turned to his lieutenant, "while five men are tying this savage, take the other five and lock his women in a big cell until I decide what is to be done with them."

...

The boys had been with Atupi long enough to know that he would not scold them if they commented occasionally. Three of the boys spoke at the same time. "Why did those men do that to Baracoraima, he was just...They stopped in mid-sentence when Atupi raised his hand.

"Baron Samedi—<u>God of magic and the underworld</u>—sent them to our people as a plague." Atupi had moved in, and his leathery old hands were resting between his knees as he squat near the fire. As swiftly as a mongoose strikes a snake, his hands were filled with embers and were thrown into the air to shower down upon the boys. They frantically brushed themselves as he leaped into the air. "That is how they rained death down upon all of The People. They had also made a new enemy of the mighty Arawak Cacique, Baracoraima."

His face was a mask of impassive observation as he watched the boys brushing the tiny embers from each other. "Listen now and you will see how a mighty warrior, even an Arawak warrior, can defeat his enemies." He looked intently into each of his young charge's eyes. When he finally spoke again, it was with an ominous tone—a warning. "Each of you young Carib warriors must always remember this." Atupi paused to be certain that each boy was listening, "We Caribs are the most powerful warriors on the land and sea, but never underestimate the Arawak—he too is a very powerful warrior, and will always be your enemy."

...

Lieutenant Alfonso had often seen similar treatment given to his own men, and also to many of the civilian Spaniards. Arawak servants were treated terrible by his commander, so he held his tongue and told five of the soldiers to follow him. He led them directly to the cool shady area where Baracoraima's wives had gathered to chat. They were talking to the Arawak women, who the men from a local village had brought to work for the Spaniards. "You women who came with the Arawak Cacique in the dugouts must come with me." He turned and barked orders to the others in their language, which he was fluent in. "The rest of you get to work on something, because the little general is feeling like a full size man today." He knew the captain had not learned one word of the local Arawak language in the three years that he had been on Isla de Margarita, plus he had no friends to carry the Lieutenant's bitter sarcastic comment to him. Lieutenant Alfonso often disrespected his commander when talking in the Arawak language. All of the women giggled but quickly vanished. They had all seen the little captain's temper—many times.

None of Baracoraima's people had seen the Spanish until now, but all had heard stories from others fleeing their brutality. The long shiny bayonet at the end of the musket that each Spanish soldier carried did nothing to encourage argument. All of Baracoraima's women allowed themselves to be herded into a log building with steel bars on the one tiny window beside a thick door.

Amatinu went to the window and looked at the soldier standing guard. When she spoke to him he turned and shrugged his shoulders. On her second try, he pointed to his ears then lips as he shook his head. Realizing he did not speak or understand her language, she knew she could speak to the other wives without fear. Amatinu was about to leave the window when she saw the man who had been her husband for over twenty years. Four small soldiers struggled with their load as an unconscious Baracoraima was being pulled across the compound by his legs. A very cold hand reached inside and grabbed her by the heart, but she remained silent. Amatinu realized there was nothing that she could do to help him—yet!

She watched until she saw which of the strange huts he was placed in, and then she turned away. "Come to me." Each of the women had long ago realized that her word was law, so they all immediately gathered around the old woman—old to them. "All of you must do as I say, or we will all die in these silly houses of the men who are now our captors." In the darkness of the room, lit by only one very small window, they could still see her intense dark eyes as she slowly turned to each. "Bukuru, Butubi." She spoke their names softly.

"Yes mama." Each and every one of Baracoraima's very young wives addressed her as mama, and looked up to her as if she was indeed their mother.

"Come with me." She headed toward the rear, and was obediently followed by the two young girls. "Sit," she said quietly, and joined them on the dirt floor. "I do not understand why, but we are now prisoners of these men. They have taken Papa (Baracoraima was called papa by all wives and many others of his village) to a small place like this one we are in. Shhhh," she hissed quietly when they gasped. "His life and our own will depend on our actions. You are the two strongest paddlers, so it is you that must go with me when we can get free."

Before she could continue, the two youngest wives, who were barely beyond the age of children themselves, said quietly, "Where are we going?"

"Somehow we will get free, and then paddle the small Carib canoe to the big island that these white men call Venezuela, and tell the Arawak men there what has happened."

"Will they come and rescue papa, and all of the other women?"

"Yes," she said confidently, "he is the greatest cacique among all of the Arawak people. They will come for him in numbers as many as the ants on the ground when food is dropped." She then paused a moment and breathed deeply before speaking again. "What I will tell you now will be frightening, but you must be strong and listen, so you can tell the other wives." She looked first to one, then the other before continuing. "These men will want you in their bed. They have many women from the big island to do the work, so it is the only reason they are keeping us like this. You must help the others understand that we will all pretend that we are hungry for these strange men's bodies. We will all do anything the silly little men tell us that they desire, and act as though we are enjoying it too." She leaned toward each, "Do you understand?"

"I think so," said Butubi, "if they think we enjoy them in the bed then they will let us walk free around this big camp."

The old woman reached out and squeezed the young girl's hand, "I have told papa many times that you are the smartest wife that he has ever had." She grinned adding, "Except me."

"I am smart too," said Bukuru.

"Yes Bukuru, you are smart, and can tell stories to the children so well they believe them. They often cannot sleep because they look for spiders as big as papa that you tell them about." When Bukuru remained silent, Amatinu continued. "You must teach the young wives how to act out their stories, and convince these men that they want to stay here with them forever."

"How long will they keep us in this dark place?"

"Long enough for us to be ready to do what they tell us."

"Are you frightened like we are?"

"Yes child," she said, and put her arm out in the near darkness to pat the girl's arm. "We are all frightened, but we must all do our best if we are to free Baracoraima." Her black eyes burned with the ferocity of a caged animal. "We will make these men wish they had never set eyes upon us. Now go to the others and tell them what they must do. I will watch from the little hole with the hard sticks on it.

3

~ War Fleet ~

Baracoraima's mind was already beginning to clear up, even before the soldiers left the jail cell. He raised his head as they departed through the door, but dark blurs was all he saw moving. He let his head fall back to the dirt floor as the door closed. *What kind of crazy men have I come to do business with?* Even thinking made his head pound worse, so he lay silent in the near-darkness and alternated between squeezing his eyes tight, then slowly opening them.

As he lay quietly in the dark, trying to clear his head and regain his strength, the man who had him imprisoned was in his office talking to his subordinate.

"Do not give that giant savage cannibal a single bite to eat or a taste of water until I tell you." He stared down from his raised desk at Lieutenant Alfonso. "Is that understood?"

"Yessir, but I've been told that he is a very powerful man among his people, and if he should die there might be some very severe repercussions."

"Lieutenant," Captain Bolivar leaned far forward as he spoke, "if those savages decide to attack this island fortress we will exterminate them as we do the flies and bugs that bother us." A sinister grin spread across his chiseled, childlike face, and his cruel black eyes penetrated the tall thin Spaniard standing at attention. "By the millions if it ever becomes necessary," he added, and then dismissed the lieutenant.

By the time that Lieutenant Juan Cortez Alfonso arrived outside the cell into which Baracoraima had been dragged unconscious, the old Arawak warrior was leaning against the wall right next to the tiny, barred window. He listened intently, but the rapid words spoken by the two men outside sounded like the monkeys chattering in the trees near his village.

"The captive," began the lieutenant, "is not to have a scrap of food or a drop of water until I myself personally bring you orders stating otherwise." He affixed the sentry with his deep blue eyes, passed on to him by his Castilian ancestors. "Those are the orders of the Commandant," he paused, "do you understand?"

"Yessir," the guard replied sharply, as he stood at rigid attention near the door.

Lieutenant Alfonso looked intently into the young Spaniard's dark eyes and said quietly, "I do not know what our glorious little commander has in his warped mind, but do not let anything happen to this savage, or you will probably pay with your own life." He continued staring a moment before adding, "Do you thoroughly understand the importance of guarding this captive?"

"Yessir!"

"Very good." He turned and left without saying another word.

Even the lowest among the fort's Spanish soldiers knew that their commander was an incompetent, egotistical fool, and most thought him totally insane as well. The young soldier's thoughts were perplexing, *why did that silly little captain treat this native like an enemy when he came to do business? Shit! Now I will never get one of those women. We will be lucky if we are not attacked when his people find out what has happened to him. We will probably all be eaten.* Few of the invading Spaniards had any knowledge about the type of people they were attempting to conquer. Most thought that all of the local natives were cannibals.

Baracoraima was still sore where the rifle butts had landed, but his mental facilities quickly returned to normal. *Could these strange people also be cannibals like the Carib? Maybe they are keeping us for food?* He could find no logic to the actions of the Spaniard, so his mind sought answers that made no sense. *Perhaps he wants to hold me ransom for women? I can have a thousand women sent to him if that is what he wants. I must study him to learn his weakness—then kill him when I have the opportunity.*

. . .

The women had been free for two weeks, but Amatinu had still not been able to talk with Baracoraima. The native women, who had long been in the fort working for the Spanish, could speak their language, so they kept her informed. "Baracoraima is being fed and watered by our people and is healthy, but he doesn't know why the captain has not come to him."

"Please have your man keep getting the water and strips of dried fish to him."

"Yes! And Amatinu," the Arawak woman paused to stare hard at the woman she had known only a short time, "my Spanish man says that many will fight against the captain and the men who will stand with him, if they will be allowed to live with the Arawak people."

Baracoraima's oldest wife stared intently for a moment at the young Arawak woman before answering. "Can you trust the words that come from this man that you live with?"

"Yes! He has been with me two years and treats me better than any man ever has. He wants to live with us and never return to his land." She paused because she was aware that if her words were carried to the captain, she would be killed. "Many of them have been thinking about killing their crazy leader, because he treats our people so bad and his own people also. They are afraid that a war fleet of our people will come from the big island and kill them all."

"And you believe they are serious?"

"Yes, but they know that the big canoes full of their Spanish people will come and learn what happened." She looked pleadingly at Amatinu, "He is a good man, and there are many more good ones who could teach our people much if we let them come and live in our villages."

Amatinu looked deep into the woman's eyes. "You are very brave to trust me with this kind of information. Let me think about it until tomorrow, and then at this same time we will talk again." She put her arms around the pretty young Arawak girl and whispered, "We will defeat the evil ones, and help those who help us free our cacique."

The girl smiled asking, "Is he really Baracoraima? I was told that he was killed before the mountains grew tall?"

"Yes, it is the mighty Baracoraima. Mortal men cannot

kill him. Only Baron Samedi can take him." When she saw the fear in the girl's eyes, she smiled saying, "Baracoraima is kind and good to all, except those who harm him or his people—and those he will destroy."

When she met with the young Arawak servant the following day, she made certain that no ears were close enough to hear. "A large war fleet will soon come to free Baracoraima. Tell your lover that every man and woman who wishes to fight against this captain and his men must keep some of the ghost-dance powder nearby at all times." She paused to watch the girl's face a moment. "Do you know how to make the powder?"

"Yes."

"Then make enough for all of the men who will fight with us. Be sure that they have it in a small pouch around their neck always. When our warriors arrive, tell everyone to wet it and smear it all over their face. I will tell the warriors that they are our friends and are helping us." She stared hard again. "Be very careful child because if this information falls into the wrong ears it will mean death for all."

"Yes Amatinu, I will tell my man to tell only those he trusts with his life."

Amatinu walked away thinking, *I must go alone to the island in the small Carib dugout. The men would miss the two young girls, and the captain will be alerted.* Her mind was full of clouds as she thought of the ordeal she must soon face alone. *An old woman like me will not be missed for a while. I must go tonight while the weather is good.* Her mind was recalling the stories that her father and uncles told of trips to this island. It was before the Spanish invaded it and slaughtered all of the Arawak Indians living here. *As soon as it is dark I will take the small Carib canoe, which is still on the bank by the river. I can make it to Isla Coche by tomorrow. The sun will shine bright, and make the clouds above the island green to guide me.* She said a silent prayer request to Olokum. *Please make me strong Mighty Olokum, so I can save Baracoraima.* She pondered her predicament a moment then added, *if the big canoe with men in iron clothes is coming—please sink it.*

. . .

An event to forever be unknown to Amatinu was occurring several hundred miles away. A Spanish Galleon, the San Carlos Emanuel, and two small but very fast Corvettes, the Ballesteros and the San Jose Maria, had been dispatched from Spain. It was heading to the very same island where Baracoraima was now being held as a hostage. They were attempting to navigate the Windward Passage between Cuba and Haiti when a freak storm drove them upon rocks in the middle of the night. The few survivors were later quoted as saying, "The sky was clear and the sea was very calm, but suddenly everything went crazy."

Had Olokum answered her prayer?

As Amatinu awaited the cover of darkness to conceal her movements, she thought, *Olokum has always blessed my family, and I am certain that he will help me now.*

It would be long after the coming events before a Spanish ship would arrive.

. . .

The guard on the following night was a very good friend of the young Arawak girl's Spanish man. He kept his eyes searching the darkness of the fort as she spoke quietly to Baracoraima in her language.
   "...and Amatinu has already gone in the small canoe?"
   "Yes!" The girl answered, "She quietly left when it was dark yesterday."
   "And you think there will be many of these strange men who will fight with us?" Baracoraima kept his powerful voice low.
   "Yes! More than both hands twice. One will come to open this house when it is time."
   "Very good, child, go now so you do not get caught."
   "Okay, but first I must let this soldier have my body."

"Make him be quiet and fast"

"They are not like the Arawak men. It takes only a brief moment to make them happy." She went to the guard and touched him, then lifted her skirt and bent over the nearby chair so he could enter her from behind. Moments later she was slipping through the darkness toward her man's room.

. . .

Atupi knew that this was an exciting time in his story, so while straddling a log seat he became more animated than usual. "Ungh, umph, ungh, umph," he panted hard as he imitated Amatinu's lonely voyage as she paddled. The tiny island, which she paddled furiously toward, lay less than ten miles from the river she would exit from. He abruptly stopped and looked at the boys sitting across from him. "Who among you has paddled a dugout alone through the ocean with the enemy behind you?"

He looked from one boy to the other, but not a word was uttered by a one of them. His voice rose as he spoke. "Soon, one of you will understand how Amatinu felt as she paddled alone, not knowing if the enemy following to kill her was gaining."

One boy was so caught up in the story that he blurted out, "She is an old woman. How can she ever get away?" The other four boys silently pondered the meaning of their teacher's statement.

Atupi's voice was now a loud scream as he jumped into the fire, waving his paddle, "A terrible enemy in pursuit of you will make you paddle faster than you now believe possible." He was back out of the coals in an instant but the image of him standing in the fire screaming would remain with the boys. Although forbidden, each had heard small hints from the older boys about the final trial at sea. Even Podomani, as young as he was, became apprehensive about the coming days.   . . .

Amatinu's voyage was uneventful. By the time the sun was above the eastern horizon, she was beyond the eyes of all on Isla de Margarita. When her old arms became tired of paddling she thought about Baracoraima—*my cacique is alone in the tiny dark room.* It refreshed her and she paddled even more ferociously, like a woman obsessed—she was.

Long before noon, the sun was high enough to bounce its light from the green trees on Isla Coche, to be reflected on the clouds above. She was proud that she could remember the teachings of her father, as he drew pictures in the sand. He told her of the stars to follow—the places they would visit for bartering—how to use the signs of Mother Nature to navigate on an open ocean.

Before she was close to the small island, several war canoes were heading toward her. When they arrived and saw that it was one of Baracoraima's old wives, they put four young boys in her dugout to paddle. A warrior sliced the top from a green coconut so she could drink the clear water, then scoop out the sweet gelatin-like mush into her mouth. When she told them what had occurred at the Spanish fort, their old cacique took immediate action. He instructed the young warriors in two of the dugouts to immediately begin the journey toward Peninsula de Araya, on the coast of Venezuela. "Tell them to assemble a very large war fleet and come to my village." With a wave of his arm they were paddling furiously south. Their journey was across a wide expanse of open sea. The young Arawak warriors had dreamed of war with the iron men since they were boys—their journey would be swift.

~ Spaniards ~

Old Amatinu was exhausted, so she sat silently in the dugout with her head hanging between her knees. As the young warriors who paddled her canoe followed the others, she thought about all of the horrible things that could happen to Baracoraima before a war party could be assembled. *Please Loa; watch over our mighty cacique until we can free him from the evil men in shiny clothes.*

When they arrived on Isla Coche, Amatinu was escorted to their small village to await the arrival of the war fleet. A week would be required to assemble the men and canoes, plus choose warriors who had fought the Spaniards in past battles. They would be needed to lead the various groups who would attack the Spanish fort from different landing places on Isla de Margarita.

The old cacique came quietly, and sat beside Amatinu. "Baracoraima has been my friend since we were children playing with wooden swords and chasing the girls of our village into the forest. Even then we all knew that he would one day become a great cacique, because of the way he treated everyone with great honor. Most of the young boys treated the girls as though they were toys to be played with and then tossed aside, but not Baracoraima. He was huge and powerful, even as a young boy, and could easily have put a girl on each of his broad shoulders and carried them into the woods to do as he chose with them."

The old cacique smiled when he saw how intensely Amatinu was listening to his story about the man she had loved nearly all of her life. "Ha, ha, ha, such good memories. It is a great wonder that my old brain has not lost them all to the many passings of the bright round moon. I, like all of the other young boys, would be long at the fires in our village when Baracoraima would return from the forest holding the hand of a maiden. She would have a face that had been touched by Aida Wedo—Goddess of rainbows—and the rainbow of happiness would be in her eyes." He turned and smiled at her.

"Yes!" Amatinu answered with eyes no longer so sad. "I was one of those young maidens. When Baracoraima loves a woman, the bright day could pass into the dark night and still he would be finding new places on a woman's body to touch and ignite the fire again."

The old man looked deeply into her eyes and shook his head slowly up and down. "I will go now and instruct my wives to begin preparing a feast to offer sacrificial pigs to Loa. She will keep him safe until the war fleet is being led by Ogoun to free the mighty Baracoraima." He turned to her before standing. "We will eat fish and cassava bread and drink cassava beer, but all of the pigs we have in pens will be sacrificed to the gods." After standing, the cacique looked down at Amatinu. "You will soon be happy again, and have Baracoraima back by your side."

After the sacrificial feast, Amatinu went to the beach before each dawn to await the sun and search the horizon for any sign of the approaching war fleet, which hopefully would free her beloved cacique.

"Old woman."

Amatinu turned when she heard a voice weakened with age. In the near dawn, a very old man was standing so close behind her that she could touch him. He was naked with the exception of a steel helmet. In his weathered old hands he held a very long sword. She immediately recognized him as the village medicine man, but had never spoken to him. She remained silent, knowing that he had come to her so early for a reason. She waited for him to speak.

"Many of our warriors will arrive today with Legba—<u>God of the Sun</u>—and you will go with them to free the mighty Cacique Baracoraima. Loa came to me in the night with a message from her son, Loa Mombu. Yayjaba has instructed Loa Mombu to guard you during the voyage to the strange men. You will pierce the heart of the evil one as he prepares to send the mighty Baracoraima to live in darkness with Baron Samedi."

Amatinu did not doubt for a moment that the old man had seen the warriors, while in a powerful trance—she knew they would soon arrive. She had listened to stories of his visions, told by the old men around the evening fire, as they drank cassava beer and smoked.

"I was once a great cacique like your man, but I am now old, and must have my meat chewed for me by my wives. Everyone in my village was killed or taken as slaves by the men in shiny clothes—I alone escaped into the jungle. I took only three things with me. The life of a man in shiny clothes—his shiny iron head dress—and his long knife." He raised the Spanish sword, placed it on his palms and held it toward Amatinu. "You will use this to save your cacique."

He placed the sword on her upraised palms, and then without another word he turned and headed back toward the village. She stood holding the sword, and watched him limping slowly away into the rapidly approaching sunrise, with the Spaniard's steel helmet resting on his withered old shoulders. She lowered the heavy weapon until the tip touched the sand and shell beach.

When the sun's glare hurt her eyes, Amatinu turned to scan the southern horizon. She was both delighted and amazed to see a war fleet larger than any which had ever been assembled by the Arawak Indian Nation. It was so large that it appeared to her as though the entire land was moving toward her. In awe, she remained motionless for several very long minutes...thinking...pondering—wondering, *how do the old medicine men see the things that will happen?*

The rescue of Baracoraima from the evil men in tin clothes would live forever in the legends of his people—as would the bravery of his woman, Amatinu.

. . .

Baracoraima lifted his head from the dirt floor when he heard the sound of approaching boots. He had reached out in the darkness, after the last visit only two days earlier, and ran his finger along the grooves that he scratched after each sunrise into the earthen floor he sat upon. *Two days more than the changing of the moon. I hope sharks did not eat old Amatinu before reaching Isla Coche.* He smiled wide in the darkness as the huge wooden door squeaked opened. *No! They would spit out that tough old woman.*

Two soldiers stepped inside with torches, and checked the room. Four more entered and grabbed the old cacique, lifting him from the floor to stand facing Captain Bolivar, who pompously strutted in wearing his full-dress uniform, heavy with medals—which he had awarded himself.

The tiny soldier looked up at Baracoraima, who had to stoop so his head wasn't touching the ceiling, and then said to his lieutenant, "Put him on his knees."

A nod from Lieutenant Alfonso brought up two of the guard's boots to the rear of the warrior's knees, forcing him to kneel. Captain Bolivar turned to his lieutenant again, and simply nodded toward the open door. Two guards entered holding one of the old cacique's very young wives between them. She was barely conscious, with numerous bruises and wounds from one end of her small bronze body to the other. Another nod from the Captain, and they dragged her from the small cell as another Indian entered.

Captain Bolivar turned to the young Arawak who had worked at the fort since its construction. The Indian spoke good Spanish and could interpret each word correctly. "Tell him that I will teach him how to approach his conqueror, so that the next time," he paused and crossed his short arms across the child-like medal-covered chest, and glared down at his captive, "if there is a next time that he comes to ask favors of his master. Perhaps then we can do business."

Baracoraima silently listened to the interpreter, and then spoke calmly. "Tell him that when I come to his house again it will be to feed him to the sharks."

The interpreter turned to Captain Bolivar, "He said he is sorry that he did not show proper respect for the mighty chief that you are."

Even on his knees, Baracoraima was still looking almost straight at the Captain. The confidence in the old man's eyes infuriated the Captain, so he nodded toward the two guards holding his arms. Each stepped back, lifted their boots, and kicked him in the back of the head. The blow sent him face down to the floor, and they quickly grasped his arms again.

When their commander turned to head out the door, they released Baracoraima's arms and followed Captain Bolivar.

When Baracoraima heard the sound of his door's latch being re-fastened, he sat once again and leaned against the wall. He thought, *even their kicks against my head are like those of the children in my village when we wrestle. They are a weak people and will be easily defeated.*

...

After the sun fell into the distant mountains on that very same late afternoon, six of the smaller inter-island Arawak dugout canoes approached the island. They arrived on the opposite side of the deep-water port. The Spanish fort was constructed on the other side, so the falling sun would have been shining directly into the Spanish soldier's eyes as the warriors approached the island. Their dugout canoes were small and fast, carrying only four warriors in each. All had been chosen for their strength and endurance, and they were all skilled guerrilla fighters who had spied on the Spaniards in Venezuela, prior to their move to Isla Coche.

The dugout canoes were hidden, and the two-dozen men immediately began the arduous ten-mile trek through the dense jungle surrounding the bay. As dawn washed the shadows from the sky, twenty exhausted men slept, as four looked down on the enemy's fort. Four men later relieved the guards so they could get some rest, then four others later relieved them. By nightfall all were rested and ready to infiltrate the fort. They were given orders to accomplish one task only, and then return to the hills and watch for the approach of the war party, which was due to arrive in two days. Their main mission accomplished, they waited, and carefully watched the activity inside the fort. Each man had made mental notes detailing every aspect of the fort's inner building locations, so that they could move swiftly through it when the time came to attack.

...

Baracoraima's eyes opened from a shallow sleep. When in the presence of his enemies he had long ago trained himself to sleep or rest for very short periods only. He lay silently thinking...motionless—waiting. Another tiny pebble struck nearby and he arose, to move silently across the darkened room to the small barred opening in the thick log door.

"They are coming tomorrow night, papa."

He recognized the soft voice of his thirteen-year-old wife, Lonatti. "Are you alone?" He whispered.

"Yes! The guard is in the bushes with Bukuru."

"How do you know that they come?"

"Men came from their village to tell us. Many of the iron men are going to join us, and then live in our villages. They will mark their faces with white ghost-dance paste, so our warriors will see it and know that they are with us." She reached through the iron bars, "Here is food, so that you can be strong when they arrive."

Baracoraima groped in the darkness until he touched the food, wrapped and tied in banana tree leaves. "I have it, now go swiftly so you are not seen." He sat in the corner where very little light, even on a bright day, entered his cell. He ate the food as he thought about the coming battle. Moments later he heard the returning guard settling back into the wooden chair beside the door. He soon heard the man drinking and thought; *Bukuru brought the guard cassava beer so he will not be alert.* Baracoraima smiled, *I hope you do not have your face marked white tomorrow night, because you will be worth nothing in our villages.*

He went across to the other far corner, and ten minutes of digging with the stone tool, which Bukuru included with his first food brought a month earlier, and he soon had the green banana leaves buried near the others. *Their foolish little cacique must think I am staying alive on the rotten fish and sip of water that he sends to me every two days.*

· · ·

The cacique in the village on Isla Coche was chosen to lead the attack on the Spanish fort. All of the other war chiefs, who had arrived from the mainland with their warriors, agreed that he was the best man for the task. "You have been to the white men's fort many times, and know how best to attack." He sat with the dozen leaders, each having brought five sixty-foot-long dugout war canoes, and thirty warriors to fill each.

All of their canoes were made from the gommier tree, which were the only trees in the jungle large enough to make stable seagoing dugouts and smaller but sturdy inter-island pirogues.

After explaining his strategy to send half of the war fleet to the place where his guerrilla scouts had landed, the old cacique paused to allow comment. After each leader had nodded his assent, he continued. "They will arrive tonight at dark, and will see the signal fires of my scouts to lead them into the river. The canoes will be hidden in the jungle when the river is no longer wide enough to continue, and they will begin the trip to the fort on foot. When the sun starts to climb from the water, they will be looking down upon the fort. The rest of us will approach the main harbor during darkness, and will be ready when Baracoraima's women have their men open the gate."

He paused to allow them all time enough to absorb what he had said before continuing. "My scouts have returned to tell me that many of the men who wear the shiny clothes will fight with us, and then live as we do. They do not like their cacique and fear that he will get them all killed if they do not join us." He smiled when one of the warriors commented how correct the Spanish soldiers were. "They will have ghost-dance paint on their face so that we can tell which of them is with us—all other men in shiny clothes must die." He turned when he heard his oldest wife call him to say that the war feast was ready. Turning back to the group of war caciques he spoke briefly. "We have all seen what these men can do with the small boom sticks they carry, and the big ones that are placed around their forts. Baracoraima's women will take the fort's men to bed each night with much cassava beer, and we will silently approach in the darkness and surprise them." With a wave of his arm he invited them all to join him as his warriors prepared to begin the ghost dance, which would allow any fallen warriors to continue on to the afterlife.

Each Arawak village had its own way of performing the dance, but all followed the ancient rule that only drums be used as the whitened warriors silently performed their dance. Amatinu never tired of watching the men gracefully spin and twirl as they kept silent rhythm with the drums. She could see their lips moving, and knew that each warrior was praying to Ogoun and asking that Baracoraima survive until they arrived. As the muffled drums transmitted their primordial sounds, she thought of all the people in her life that had fallen in battle and gone on to the afterlife. She said a silent prayer to Ghede; *please let Baracoraima stay here with us.*

The war feast that his entire village had been preparing was ready, and all of the warriors ate heartily, knowing that it might be their last meal or at least their last for quite a while.

By noon, the feast was over and the fleet prepared to depart. The first six caciques led their war canoes toward the area on Isla de Margarita, opposite the fort's location. This first group of thirty war canoes carried over nine hundred seasoned warriors, and would be met by the guerrilla scouts who would lead them across the island to the fort. An hour later, the remaining thirty canoes departed Isla Coche carrying a similar number of warriors. In the lead dugout sat Amatinu—sword in hand. Their voyage would be much farther, because they had to pass between Isla Cubagua and Isla de Margarita, and then continue north until they rounded the tip. The fleet would then skirt the island until the small signal fire informed the men that the harbor was just around the corner.

Guabancex was appreciative for the sacrifice of pigs and goats; the fleet was blessed with calm seas. The voyage still required skilled seamanship by these small bronze men who were unsurpassed throughout the world of water. A small warrior could touch both sides of the canoe at the same time—often during long voyages across seas with waves fifteen-feet tall.

Fifty miles away at the fort on Isla de Margarita, Captain Christopher de Cordova Bolivar, and the majority of his disgruntled group of slightly over five hundred Spanish soldiers, and all of his officers, was in serious trouble and completely unaware. All but a few of the soldiers were without a small amount of white face paint in a tiny pouch hanging unseen from their neck. In the absence of complete trust, their comrades did not inform them. They did not want them living on the islands that they soon planned to call home for the balance of their lives.

More than eighteen hundred vengeful Arawak warriors were now en route to rescue their beloved, legendary, Cacique Baracoraima. Each had a family story of suffering at the hands of the cruel Spaniards. Either they or their loved ones had learned first hand about the sadistic brutality of these men who wore shiny clothes. Every warrior carried a personal hatred and looked forward to the coming battle.

. . .

More that four-thousand-miles away, and a month earlier, another fleet was being assembled on the coast of Spain. The small fleet of resfuerzos—<u>supply ships</u>—was being loaded with supplies and soldiers, to relieve the men on Isla de Margarita and other small Caribbean and South American outposts. The fleet's Admiral, Diego de Nunez was in Seville receiving his orders.

"After discharging your troops and supplies at the various forts along the coast, you will continue on to our settlement of Caracas in New Spain. While our many naos—<u>merchant ships</u>—are being re-fitted for the perilous journey home, the patches—<u>re-con ships</u>—will be south, loading gold and silver. When your ballast stones have all been replaced with the treasure they bring, you are to lead your fleet to Cuba and prepare for the run home to Mother Spain."

After issuing orders to Vice Admiral Alonzo Alvara de Pineza, the fleet of forty-three vessels headed west toward the Azores. Here is where they would enter the waters of the Mid Atlantic Ridge, and then turn toward the land they were calling New Spain, which would eventually become South America.

Had this Spanish fleet arrived on time to relieve Captain Bolivar's long-suffering troops, the severe consequences to the Arawak Indian war fleet coming to rescue Cacique Baracoraima would have been catastrophic.

The whims of Mother Nature have often altered the course of history. She now decided not to smile down on the Spaniards.

~ She was siding with the Arawak war fleet ~

After rounding the Azores, Admiral Nunez and his fleet enjoyed one day of fair weather. During the night, their sails stiffened and the masts holding them braced against a cold wind that came rushing down toward them from Davis Strait to their north.

Soldiers and civilian passengers slept, as the Admiral and his seasoned seamen watched with apprehension and concern at the building seas—and wind now howling like crazed banshees. The following dawn found the ships running beneath stretched canvas and stressed sticks, as though each vessel was in a race with every other ship.

The northwest wind hit Newfoundland at gale force, and then entered the North Atlantic Ocean—roaring south like an insane pride of lions. Many miles north of the Arawak war fleet, a battle would soon begin between wood, canvas, iron fittings, and steel-hard seamen. Each was being pitting against the two most powerful combined forces on earth—wind and water.

. . .

The first group of warriors arrived on Isla de Margarita, and was met by the guerrilla scouts. Their dugouts were concealed near the rivers that they were led into by very small, shielded signal fires. With little noise and no talking, they began the journey across the island toward the fort. All had at one time or another battled the Spaniards near their original homes along the coast of South America, and were aware of their enemy's cunning tactics. They took no chances, and sent out forward scouts, plus they also sent scouting parties far to the rear to be certain they were not being followed.

Never had so large a war fleet been assembled by the Arawak Nation. Never had there been an Arawak Cacique so deserving of their loyalty, as Baracoraima.

As they quietly moved toward the fort, the remaining fleet of thirty, sixty-foot-long dugout canoes raced across calm seas, benefiting from a slight tailwind. As violent as Mother Nature had treated the Spanish Admiral's fleet of huge modern ships in the Mid Atlantic Ridge a month earlier, she was turning a very kind eye toward the small bronze-skinned warriors crossing the sea in their hand hewn dugout canoes. They were now rounding the tip of the small Caribbean island where Baracoraima was being held prisoner.

Had Admiral Diego de Nunez only departed Spain two days earlier, his fleet of ships would have missed the violent northwester. He would have arrived on time at Captain Bolivar's fort, and the Arawak Indians would have walked into a situation from which few would have survived.

HOWEVER

The thirty canoes slipped silently into the harbor, and following the directions of Amatinu, they made their way easily into the many small canals that went into the central jungles of the island. With their vessels well hidden, the warriors stealthily moved toward the fort. As the Captain slept soundly, dreaming of a grandeur life of prestige and leisure in Spain, his guards drank cassava beer, and wallowed nakedly in sexual splendor with Baracoraima's young wives. Not one of nearly a thousand Arawak warriors was heard or seen as they silently assembled on each side of the fort's huge wooden gates.

. . .

Admiral Diego de Nunez, and the remaining vessels of his fleet, began re-assembling after the storm passed. Of the forty-three ships that departed Spain with the Admiral, thirteen were never seen again including the Almiranta—<u>vice flagship</u>, three armed galleons, and five naos. All were lost, but worse than all of the others combined, was the loss of three resfuerzos, and their precious cargo of supplies. The forts in the new settlements depended upon these fresh supplies for their survival.

The huge vessel, Capitana—<u>fleet flagship</u>, had suffered severely damaged rigging, but was able to limp on slowly through calm seas, as the crew worked around the clock making repairs. Within two weeks, the Admiral's pataches had scouted to great distances, and located four resfuerzos, nine galleons and one nao. The ten pataches that left with the Admiral, remained intact and nearby during the storm. Their smaller size and maneuverability made them much less vulnerable to the high winds and huge seas. They now worked in two groups to locate the scattered ships. When one or more was located, they guided them back to the Capitana.

After the remaining twenty-three ships were together again and repaired, they continued toward their main destination. Eventually the fort on Isla de Margarita was reached—but very late. What they found waiting there was forever indelibly imprinted on every man's mind.

5

~ Enemy Inside ~

Several of the advance scouts easily entered the fort within an hour of arriving. Their nearly naked body's bronze skin blended perfectly with the wooden buildings and aged posts of the fort walls. After silently lowering themselves on woven honeysuckle vine ropes, they stood absolutely quiet and motionless until their eyes had become accustomed to the shadows inside the fort. In less than an hour they had located each sentry who was drinking cassava beer, and fornicating with Baracoraima's young wives. Each Arawak warrior held a wire-like garrote, also made of honeysuckle vine, between two short pieces of mahogany. The success of this mission depended on the silent death of the guards. They stood in the shadows waiting for the signal that would come an hour before dawn—if all went well with the second half of their fleet. If the signal didn't come, their orders were to silently leave the fort and wait another day.

Amatinu stood at the gate and watched as the young warrior easily climbed the fiber rope to the top of the fort's log wall. Moments later she heard the trilling sound coming from his lips, and prepared herself by gripping the sword's handle firmly.

The scouts, standing only an arm's length from drunken guards mounted atop the women, heard the trilling and instantly began a practiced count to ten. When their silent count reached ten, all eight warriors stepped silently forward and slipped the garrote over the errant guard's head. Instantly the vine sliced deeply into his neck, cutting off all air and sound. A knee in the back, plus the assistance of the Arawak women, prevented all useful movement by the drunken guards. A few seconds of futile thrashing—a few more of quivering hands digging for the garrote—seconds of spastic stiffening—one minute more—motionless...all died silently.

Amatinu was the first person inside when young Lonatti and her Spaniard lover opened the gate. The young girl spoke quietly to her older mentor, as she pointed toward a nearby building. "There are many of the Spanish soldiers with ghost-dance paint on their faces. They are gathered near the building where papa is being held prisoner. They have a big log that they will use to break down the door when it is time."

"Good," Amatinu replied, "go to them and say that they must wait until the buildings are all ablaze, so the noise will not matter, then free papa." She then followed the men who were carrying turtle shells with sand in them and filled with smoldering embers, tended carefully during the voyage. Others carried bundles of dry fibers that had been stashed near the fort's entrance by the advance scouts. Several other warriors carried armloads of dry wood, which had also been stashed by the scouts for their use.

The cacique from the Isla Coche village stayed near Amatinu from the moment she stepped from his canoe. He whispered to her now in the darkness, "Our scouts say that all of the doors are now held closed with poles, and there are no windows where they sleep, so they cannot escape." He nudged her arm and pointed to a two-story building. "They say that the cacique lives in the room near the steps on this end," he pointed toward the eastern end, "and his war chiefs live in the other rooms that lead to the western steps. They feared waking them if they went up to bar the doors, so they will come out when the flames and screaming begins."

"We will be waiting for them with smiles on our face and weapons in our hands," Amatinu said then quickly gathered together two-dozen warriors, and led them to the stairs leading up to Captain Bolivar's private quarters. Since his officer's quarters were also located along the balcony of the same long building, warriors silently moved into position. As they began stealthily going up the steps, they saw that the flames were already building all around the many buildings that housed all of the soldiers. She remembered watching as the cruel little man entered his private living quarters, after strutting along behind her man as he was dragged to his cell. She motioned for the others to go to the doors of the other six rooms. Amatinu held the huge sword and waited. Less than one hour after the Arawak warriors entered the fort, it was ablaze.

The sleeping quarters were so tightly packed that panic caused many of the Spaniards to be trampled by their fellow soldiers, as they frantically tried to break down the door. It was held in place by pointed poles stuck into the floor, and lodged against the door. They were held by sturdy Arawak warriors—the soldier's efforts were futile.

Captain Bolivar heard the screaming of his men, and what to him sounded like crackling flames. Still in his long nightshirt, he flung open his door to find an old woman holding a sword. A look of disbelief crossed his face as the sword was shoved deep into his stomach. "Hold tightly," Amatinu screamed as he gripped the blade. "Maybe you can keep me from pulling it out." She placed her foot on his thin sunken chest and shoved. His grip tightened as he stared into her eyes. The hatred Amatinu felt, radiated toward him along with the blaze of the building. Fingers fell as he landed against the door's opening. "Ha," she laughed, "you did no better holding the blade than my mother did." He could do nothing but hold his fingerless hands to the hole in his stomach as she raised the blade above her head. He closed his eyes a moment before it landed against his face—repeatedly. As he slipped toward the floor she drew the blade across his throat, then turned and ran the blade through another man in a nightshirt. He was holding a sword above his head, about to strike a warrior that was battling another soldier who was standing naked with a pistol in his hand.

The remaining six officers were easily slaughtered as they rushed from their quarters. Amatinu saw the flames below, and knew that this building had also been torched. She yelled, and motioned toward the stairs. When her bare feet touched dirt, she ran immediately toward the building where Baracoraima was imprisoned. She was happy to see him standing—a head taller than the others and looking like the stoic warrior that always filled her pleasant dreams.

Baracoraima smiled when he saw her running at him. "So old woman, you came to free your old cacique."

She stopped to catch her breath as she leaned very casually on the sword, and said with a big smile, "No! I brought this weapon to you so you could free yourself, but as always you slept through the battle." She handed the sword to him.

"Ah! Yes." He lifted the first sword he ever held. "It is a good weapon, and I will use it, but I must make another war club to make my wives behave." He smiled slightly as he hefted the weapon. "I fear that this might make them useless and unable to work."

Amatinu stepped close and put her arms around his waist then laid her head against his chest. "I will go into the forest and locate the best ironwood tree for you to make it from."

By dawn the screams of the soldiers being roasted alive had stopped. When the sun was directly overhead there was little left but bones and ashes inside the fort's walls. Baracoraima was now in charge, and he began issuing orders. As the warriors began work, he spoke to the other caciques gathered nearby. "The soldiers with shiny clothes who are going to live with us have told me that many ships are coming soon, so we must depart swiftly. I have told our men to impale those men who did not completely burn, and place their bodies above the ashes as though they were cooked for food." He grinned before continuing, "We will leave nothing to make them think that the Arawak people were here. They will be certain that the Carib cannibals attacked and burned this fort, and then feasted on the little white men."

One old cacique shook his head in approval, "Today we have defeated two mighty enemies."

. . .

Atupi remained silent for several minutes after telling the boys about the attack on the Spanish fort by the Arawak Indians. After so many years of telling the legend to new groups of future warriors, he knew what would be going through their young minds. He rigidly trained each group to remain silent until he was finished, so knowing that they had many questions he said, "Speak your thoughts now."

The first to speak was the son of a Carib war chief. "Did the men who wear the shiny clothes ever catch and kill Cacique Ahameke?"

"No! Many say that he too is still alive, like Baracoraima, and is still raiding the little white men in shiny clothes."

Another asked, "Did the white men in shiny clothes, who came in the big canoes, think that it was Caribs who burned the fort and ate their warriors?"

"Yes, because Baracoraima was very smart. He had the arms and legs cut from those men who did not burn, and then they busted the bones to make it look as though we wanted to get inside to the marrow. The white men have hunted us ever since."

A small boy timidly asked Atupi, "Have you eaten your enemies?"

"Yes! When I was a young warrior, my village attacked many Arawak villages. We always took one or two of the enemy to roast later as a celebration." He paused and looked hard at each young boy before continuing. "We do not eat our enemies because they taste good, or because we have no food. There are many animals in the jungle that are easier to catch or kill and every one of them tastes better than people." He paused again to ask, "Who knows why we eat our enemies?"

"To make all people fear the Carib." It was the tall muscular son of his cacique, and Atupi was pleased with his answer—he liked the boy. Atupi was certain that Atahana would one day also be a great cacique.

"Yes Atahana, and with many passings of the round moon, we are still the most feared warriors on the land or the water. Before our warriors began eating their enemies, we were just another of the many tribes living on the big island. We were ferocious and bold, but so were many others.

When they began finding what was left after our warriors celebrated a victory over their enemies, fear of the Carib people spread like blood poured into the sea. Soon entire villages ran into the jungle when word came from their scouts that we were coming. Our men would just go to a village and take what they wanted. When other warriors attacked our village, and lost the battle, the Carib Cacique would have three of their warriors tied to a tree. The other enemy warriors would be slowly roasted, and part of them eaten while they still lived. It took a very long time, and the men begged to be killed, but the celebration went on until the last one was dead. The enemy warriors would then be released to carry their story back to the other tribes. Soon, the only people who attacked us were the white invaders in shiny clothes and the Arawak."

The old teacher stood to stretch the soreness from his body, and then motioned with a nod at the fire, and the five boys ran for more wood. Atupi began stirring the embers to get flames, so the new logs would begin burning when thrown on.

The boys did not want Atupi to stop the story, so they hurried to bring enough wood. They wanted to hear what happened after the fort was burned.

When the fire was roaring and his joints ached less, Atupi leaned forward and spoke.

"The moon was only a very small piece, showing from

behind the big mountain in the sky, when the Arawak attacked the fort to free Baracoraima and kill all of the white men. They soon returned to their villages on Isla Coche and also the big island. Baracoraima went back to Trinidad with enough of the white men's steel swords and guns to make tools and construct a very large war fleet."

. . .

"Captain, captain," a Spaniard high in the rigging yelled, "I see the fort." He pointed ahead of the ship as it moved south after leaving the island of Antigua only three days earlier.

Admiral Diego de Nunez led his four resfuerzos, one nao, and two very heavily armed galleons into the harbor. His remaining galleons and pataches were running south to the Spanish settlements along the coast of South America. Their orders were to begin loading all of the gold, silver, and other treasures, stolen from the local indigenous people who they had enslaved years earlier.

His rendezvous with the fleet was to be in the Bay of Panama, as had been previously determined by meetings with his various commanders of the galleons. They had to distribute the treasure among the many vessels, and begin the trip to Cuba for outfitting and preparations for the long trip back to Spain. The horror stories, which were later told of what they saw at the fort, would send tremors of fear throughout the Spanish armada, the Caribbean islands, and the many Spanish settlements along the east coast of South America for many years to come.

The Carib Indians that they had battled along the shores of South America, and eventually pursued far into the Caribbean Sea, were no longer savages to be dealt with in a severe manner—they were now a cunning and formidable enemy to fear.

Two months later, Admiral Diego de Nunez stood on the deck of his Capitana, and watched his last two galleons enter the harbor on the north side of Cuba. The loss of his thirteen ships, so soon after majestically leaving Spain, had left him nearly despondent. He was now very pleased with the large amount of treasure aboard the galleons, reported to him by one of his pataches a week earlier.

"Yes Admiral," Captain Hernando de Camargo reported to him, after securing his patache on anchor in the harbor, "the galleons have all now replaced the ballast stones with treasure and are running toward here laying very deep in the water."

"Ah yes," the Admiral smiled, "we will all certainly receive a glorious reception when finally we arrive back home in Mother Spain."

It was August when the Admiral's fleet was repaired and fully outfitted by the Spanish craftsmen in Cuba. His unfortunate encounter with the freak storm shortly after departing Spain had delayed his fleet. The disaster he found waiting within the charred walls of the fort at Isla de Margarita further delayed him. The clear blue sky, which radiated from horizon to horizon as his fleet of thirty ships left the harbor in Cuba and moved north into the Straits of Florida to enter the Gulfstream's northerly pull, was about to change, and add to his streak of bad luck.

As the Admiral's navigator began plotting their course along the southern coast of North America, to the point where they would turn toward Spain, his eyes constantly returned to the darkening sky.

By nightfall of the second day after leaving Cuba, the glassy harbor was a disaster. Ships were being piled on top of each other as if they were toys, or flung far up onto the shore. The gently swaying palm trees were now bent so low that many brushed the ground with their fronds. Hundreds died as over two-hundred-mile-an-hour winds relentlessly battered the small island of Cuba, before moving north into the straits. They were the same waters that the Admiral's fleet had entered two days earlier.

The hurricane soon caught up with the ships, slowly plodding along toward the north. The day after that, it moved north another three hundred miles then turned inland and blew itself out. By that time the Admiral and his fleet were no more.

There was one battered galleon, and one small patache remaining of the thirty ships. All the others were scattered splinters along the sandy coral shores of the Florida Keys, and the remains of the ships were soon little more than piles of ballast stones—and treasure, waiting on the many shallow reefs for future generations of treasure salvers. There were piles of incredible treasure, which in years to come would ignite the imagination of men who dreamed of gold.

The galleon limped alone into a small harbor on the southern coast of what would soon become Florida. The crew dropped anchor to begin assessing the damage, but the jungle along the shore was full of dark watching eyes. The local Indians had encountered the Spaniards on previous voyages, and knew the kind of treatment they would receive if they allowed them to come ashore with their guns and swords.

As darkness pulled its shroud over the galleon and the exhausted men aboard it, one hundred small, hand-hewn war canoes full of fierce Calusa warriors paddled silently toward her.

The lone patache headed east into the Bahamas and landed safely on Grand Bahama Island. Their safety was also short lived—the Arawak Indians, who had run far north in a futile attempt to escape cruel treatment by the Europeans, slaughtered the crew, and then utilized every scrap of material from the small ship.

~ Nature had once again balanced the scales of justice ~

6

~ Trinidad War Fleet ~

Baracoraima's triumphant return to Trinidad was cause for a long, bountiful celebration. Several small canoes were carried to the leveled ceremonial area, where they were filled with palm fronds, and the women began preparing food to be placed on clay platters inside. Twenty-two of the Spanish soldiers, who sided with the Arawak, accompanied him to their new island home. It lay only a short distance off the east coast of Venezuela. The old cacique soon learned how fortuitous it was that two of these men chose to live with his people on Trinidad.

During the three day feast, there was an abundance of cassava beer, delicious foods, including an array of scale fish, turtle, sea and land crabs, lobsters, manatee, wild pigs, parrots, sweet potatoes, corn, sweet and hot peppers, a pepperpot full of boiled peanuts, a vast variety of fruits, and many lovely naked maidens swaying seductively as they danced to the mellow tones emitted from bamboo flutes. Naked warriors danced vigorously to the primal beat of skin-covered drums, and to the delight of the Spaniards now living with the Arawak Indians, a variety of athletic games began that they were all invited to participate in. Groups of Arawak warriors would choose three or four Spaniards by pointing to their favorites, and once they understood the rules, they were encouraged by cheers from the watching maidens and others who chose not to participate.

On the evening of the fourth day, the celebration was over. Baracoraima sought out the Spaniards and talked with two of them. Panlo de Narvaez told him that he had worked in a Seville foundry prior to signing on as a seaman in Captain Bolivar's ill-fated mission to construct a fort on Isla de Margarita. What he didn't know about working with iron, he said that Francisco Garay did. Francisco told Baracoraima that he had once operated a very successful blacksmith shop on the outskirts of Seville, until his pretty young wife noticed a wealthy merchant showing interest in her. When she left with the merchant, Francisco left with Captain Bolivar.

During the first day and evening of the celebration feast, Baracoraima had noticed that two of the young, unattached Arawak maidens took a keen interest in the two Spaniards. Arawak warriors loved to dance as well as the women, and once their hunger, from observing the food being prepared was finally satiated, they formed groups to dance. Many had previously learned to specialize in a wide variety of dances commonly used at their feasts, ceremonies, and the burials of their Arawak Caciques, relatives and friends.

Baracoraima was very pleased when he saw his people urging the Spaniards to get on their feet and join them as they danced. When several of them did, he smiled wide and began clapping his huge hands to the beat of the drums, flutes, and rattles. Soon there were many doing the same thing, and laughing as the girls went among the dancing Spaniards, and as a team, removed their trousers and rotting underwear. The old women had tears running down their dark cheeks as the naked Spaniards, filled with cassava beer, began shaking from side to side, as they saw the Arawak do, thereby making their limp manhood slap against their lily-white legs.

Baracoraima smiled when he spotted Arnesto Salinar and the young girl who had been with him since the feast began. They walked hand-in-hand into the forest on the first night, and he smiled again when Vasquez Molina did the same with his maiden the following night. *These men*, he thought as he sat drinking beer, *will bring new babies and new blood into the Arawak villages.*

After the feast, Baracoraima explained his dire need of tools to Panlo de Narvaez. "We must learn to shorten the time that it takes us to complete a war canoe, so that we can rid the land and water of the terrible Carib cannibals." The two Spaniards helped him choose which of the many swords that were taken from the ill-fated fort were to be distributed to his loyal warriors as weapons, and the rest would be converted to tools. Both men had been with the same two women during their entire time at the fort, and spoke the Arawak language fluently. They soon had a small group of natives scouring the island in search of material to construct a stone forge. Others were sent to kill wild pigs so that their hides could be cured to make a bellows.

Only two weeks after arriving back on his home island, Trinidad, Baracoraima watched as the leather bellows fed a stone forge. When the sword was red-hot, he was amazed to see Panlo easily re-shape it into a curved tool that could be used inside the fallen and split gommier trees to create the hull of a huge new dugout war canoe. He smiled at his new toolmaker, and then patted him on the shoulder. "Now we will go in search of enough gommier trees to build a fleet of war canoes, and defeat the Carib cannibals. The gommier trees are not as plentiful here as they are on the big island of Venezuela, but we will begin here, and when you have trained enough of my people, I will send them there to continue."

The old Arawak Cacique's eyes were aglow as he spoke to the Spaniard. "Panlo," Baracoraima rested his huge hand on the small man's shoulder and looked down as he spoke, "after you have completed training my people here to make canoe building tools from swords, would you take your woman and move to Grenada?" Without waiting for an answer, he continued. "The best gommier trees grow on that small island, and there are many good canoe builders among my people who live there." He paused in thought a moment before continuing, "Must be at least five hundred, good strong Arawak men and half that many old and very young."

Panlo looked up at Baracoraima and grinned wide, "We will first need to build us a house as soon as we arrive on Grenada," his grin was a bit wider as he continued, "we cannot have our new child living beneath banana leaves."

The huge old warrior slapped him on the back, almost knocking the small man off his feet, "Congratulations, but what took you so long?" He looked down to see Panlo's brow furrowed. "Ha, ha, ha, Amatinu told me that she is certain Francisco's seed is already growing in his woman, and she has never been wrong about this."

Panlo smiled slyly, "I have always been slow about such things," his face opened into a mischievous grin. "I take a great deal of time with such things, and seek a perfect product." The two men, absolute opposites, walked back toward the village talking and laughing like two long time friends.

Early the following day Baracoraima arrived in an area that his village's master canoe builder had chosen. The old man pointed to a gommier tree that was over five feet in diameter, and over a hundred feet tall. "See how straight the trees in this area are?" He waited as his cacique bent back and looked toward the top. When he shook his huge head, the old man continued. "These are so straight that we will split them and build two large canoes from each half." His toothless smile made Baracoraima grin.

"Who will replace you my friend?"

"I plan to live as long as you need war canoes."

"Good, then I will proceed slowly, so you will live long."

By the time cooling winds of fall began blowing across the island of Trinidad, and her much smaller neighbor Tobago, Baracoraima's plans for a large war fleet of dugout canoes was materializing. Near his village lay five of the huge gommier trees. They were all marked for boats of two different lengths. Thinner trees would be used to make the shorter, river and inter-island pirogue, and the wide longer section for the larger seagoing vessels used for long distance trading, and visiting among the Arawak people on distant islands.

The same methods used in cutting the long trees down, and then splitting them into halves, had been used for centuries. The new steel tools were now making the work proceed much faster, and could be accomplished with less labor, which pleased everyone.

Panlo de Narvaez taught several of the Arawak and three of the Spaniards, the art of foundry. Francisco Garay taught others what he knew of the blacksmith trade, and soon, tools were being used in the hands of Indians who had previously applied only primitive methods to cut down the huge, tall, gommier trees and build their canoes from them.

Axe and hatchet heads were forged from the hundreds of swords recovered from the fires at the fort. The pistols of the Spaniards trapped in their barracks were destroyed, but the steel in them was reused, and the swords that emerged undamaged, were forged into tools that became many times more valuable to the Arawak.

By the use of many small iron wedges, followed by larger hardwood wedges of varying widths, the trees soon became two pieces. Some were over sixty feet long, while others were between twenty-five and thirty. In a length of time that amazed the Indians, four sections lay ready for transport to the large cleared area near Baracoraima's village, where an organized boat-works was taking shape.

Only one canoe at a time had been painstakingly constructed previously—felled by firing the tree at its base, then hollowed out with the use of fire and primitive scraping tools. All of this required one year to complete. Twenty were now simultaneously being shaped by men eager to help, and they were completed in a period of time that the natives found hard to believe.

The old cacique gathered to him the most promising of his men, and five of the Spaniards. Under his masterful leadership he soon had a group of men who eagerly carried forward his life-long dream of a huge war fleet to defeat the Carib cannibals. Baracoraima's dream was carried to other villages, and with the help of Panlo de Narvaez, men on Grenada were soon turning out canoes faster than the natives had ever dreamed possible. Every Arawak village cacique shared his intense hatred of the domineering Carib Indians, and eagerly began searching for gommier trees suitable for use as canoes.

Through the winter, hundreds of men worked. Trees fell to regularly sharpened axes, foundries blazed hot while hammers pounded swords into wedges, adzes, axes, and scraping tools. When spring arrived there was a fleet of fifty seagoing war canoes on Venezuela, thirty on Trinidad, and forty on Grenada. No sooner were they launched into the nearby rivers, than other split gommier trees were being dragged in by hundreds of female natives, plus boys and girls who were old enough to pull, shove or push, as others continuously moved roller logs ahead for the huge trees to roll forward on.

This same scene was happening on other smaller islands. The entire Arawak Nation was alive with dreams of defeating the dreaded Carib cannibals.

. . .

Atupi was now approaching one of his own favorite parts of the story, and was please that his new group of young Carib warriors was attentive and displaying a keen interest in their people's history. The boys took turns at the fire, which held a wild pig that was captured in one of the traps that Atupi had instructed them how to build. All of the boys hungrily watched the fat drip into the fire as they took turns slowly revolving the small pig.

Atupi sat leaning against a huge old mahogany tree in the distance and silently assessed his group. *I have never had a better gathering of young warriors on this mountain. One of them will surely become a legend, just as our great ancestor, Cacique Ahameke did.*

After feasting on roast wild pig, cassava-root bread, and

sweet potatoes, all of the boys gathered close, while eating peanuts boiled in salty water to which hot peppers had been added. They listened as Atupi began the story about their legendary warrior ancestor, Cacique Ahameke.

"Stories about the death of Ahameke's son Bapatou, traveled far across the water on the breath of Guantuava. When her sad mournful words reached Ahameke, he did not mourn." Old Atupi paused to be certain that all were listening, and not still wishing that the pig had been larger, or were distracted by opening the boiled peanuts.

One boy asked, "Did he not mourn because he did not love his son, Bapatou?"

Atupi settled into the pile of leaves and soft branches that the boys had piled near the fire. He looked at tiny Uhubati as he thought, *this little boy fears all, but I believe that he will overcome his fears and become one of the fiercest warriors.*

He accepted the gourdful of cassava beer and continued. "Yes Uhubati, Ahameke loved him very much. Bapatou was the first child that he and Aketoni welcomed into the world, but he knew that he could not bring him back from the land of Ghede. As Aketoni grieved with Ahameke's other wives, he walked to the water, and spoke to Adamisil Wedo—<u>Water Goddess</u>. Ahameke asked her to carry this message to his son Bapatou."—'I will not leave the land of men until I have killed Baracoraima, or am killed myself.'

Atupi looked again at each of the five boys, now leaning far forward to hear his every word. They had all heard about the feats of Ahameke. He was the immortal standard by which all Carib warriors still measured themselves—and all of their fellow warriors.

The old teacher took a deep breath before continuing, "Ahameke knew nothing about the large war fleet that Baracoraima was building, but he understood that to cross the water from the island of Martinique, where Ahameke was living at this time, he would need larger canoes and many of them. His men immediately began selecting trees, and building fires at the bottom to drop them to the forest floor. Many Carib villages were building war canoes, but they did not have the Spaniard's knowledge of steel that Baracoraima had acquired. It would be a year before his small fleet would be ready for the trip to Trinidad to begin the search for his son's slayer. Ahameke instructed his best men to go in the smaller dugout pirogues, and move from island-to-island, until they reached Trinidad and the big land beyond. He needed more women for his men to breed with, so his numbers would grow larger, but of far greater importance to him was the need of information about his enemy's plans.

Bameeta was Ahameke's only daughter, but while she was still a child, he saw a great warrior within her. In mock combat with her brothers and the village boys, she was a fierce fighter. One boy lost an eye, another some teeth, and a third his dignity. After wrestling the boy to the ground, she grabbed his tiny penis. With her wooden knife in one hand and the boy's manhood in the other, she said loudly, "I will take this as my trophy." Only intervention by the village elders saved the boy a humiliating and painful ordeal.

He ran into the jungle screaming obscenities. "It was only a wooden knife held by a silly, crazy girl child."

"It was only practice combat." Ahameke did not look at the boy's young mother, who was standing nearby. He was staring proudly at his daughter.

The boy's mother turned and looked at Ahameke, "You are right, but I believe that she would have cut it off."

Ahameke nodded at the woman, and then looked at his daughter, who was wrestling with another, much older boy nearby. "Yes! She would have."

Bameeta was only a fifteen year old girl when Ahameke called her to him. "Your brother Bapatou was killed by the Arawak." He watched as her dark eyes narrowed, and was not surprised when she did not begin wailing like her mother and the other wives had done moments earlier when they were informed.

She spoke from between severely pinched lips. "I will avenge him, my father."

Three days later she was sitting with seven warriors in a twenty-seven-foot-long dugout canoe. Her eighteen-year-old brother, Raouti, sat in the stern with a steering paddle, and was in charge of the fleet of ten small war canoes. Before departing Martinique, his father called him to the fire where he and the village sub-chiefs were gathered.

"Continue until you reach the big island of Venezuela, where there are still many of the Arawak villages. Before beginning your trip home, get as much information as possible without being seen. You and your warriors must not be caught, because I need to know all that Baracoraima is planning, and also what the men in shiny clothes are doing. On the return trip, be very cautious as you destroy villages on the small islands. Many of the Arawak have already battled the white men and might have sentries in trees watching for their return. I need young girls brought back for our warriors to breed with, so our numbers will grow. Move unseen from island to island while gathering information, and then later, when you are heading home, destroy the Arawak villages as you find them. Take captive women for our warriors so they can make wives of them and put Carib babies in their bellies.

Raouti needed no further orders. He understood exactly what was expected of him, and began selecting the young warriors who would accompany him on the mission.

During the fifty-mile journey to St Lucia, the weather was calm. Raouti halted his fleet as soon as the island was sighted. "We will await darkness, then silently land on the beach and gather information."

Ahameke and other warriors, who had made this same voyage in years past, had instructed Raouti before leaving, "There are many small islands between Zeteena Island and Grenada, but there will be no villages on most. If you see no cooking fires, you will be able to stop there and rest, as you approach the big island of Grenada."

When Raouti landed on Grenada, and had all of his canoes hidden, he saw five more huge war canoes being built by men using the same tools as those on St Lucia. Raouti knew he had stumbled upon potentially valuable information that would help his father.

Two days later they departed, after accumulating and memorizing details that would allow Raouti and Bameeta's father, Ahameke, to defeat their enemy, the Arawak. His thoughts were of a future as a famous warrior like his father, *with the knowledge I gather on this trip, perhaps the Carib nation can run the Arawak from these islands for good. I will be remembered as the warrior who made it possible.* He smiled inwardly as he held the steering oar and guided his small vessel toward what they thought was a huge island—Venezuela.

Raouti's war fleet covered the seventy miles slowly, by traveling across the shallow banks near the islands. Raouti wanted to accumulate as much knowledge of the area as possible, so he carefully studied every aspect of the waters that he moved across. Already a wise young seaman, he used the moonlight to memorize the approaches to the small islands, in the event he required a refuge in the future from pursuit or storms. It proved to be a smart move that would be used many times in the long careers of Raouti and his sister, Bameeta.

Bameeta realized that her brother was a wise leader, and watched his every move. She would eventually become the only female Carib Cacique—the fiercest and most feared and dreaded of all.

Camped on the small island of Ronde, only several miles from Grenada, Raouti made a wise decision. "We will leave tonight, and by-pass Grenada." He held up his hand to silence several of his warriors, who were now enjoying the thrill of stealthily gathering information as the Arawak

Indians slept. "We have encountered only small villages of Arawak who were not guarded by warriors. Our Carib neighbors have told of returning from raids on the big island called Venezuela, and seeing the giant ships of the white men moving swiftly toward Grenada. Cacique Ahameke is depending on us to bring him all information possible about Baracoraima, and we must not fall into a trap where many of the strange white men might be waiting for us. There are also many Arawak warriors on Grenada, and we are small in number. Ahameke must see the new tools we will bring, so we will stop at Grenada on the way home when it is dark and see how many war canoes the Arawak there are also building." He glared at the one lone Carib warrior who continued to protest—attempting to over-ride his authority. The young warrior quickly wilted beneath Raouti's intense black eyes—and those of his sister. "I am going to take one other canoe with me and stop on the island of Trinidad to learn what the Arawak there are doing. If they are also building large war canoes, then Ahameke must be told as soon as possible."

Raouti paused and one-by-one looked into the eyes of each of his warriors, including his sister, "I tell you all this. We will return one day and deal with these Arawak pigs that are spreading like the maggots do in neglected meat."

~ Raouti keeps his promise ~

"My cacique, I have a question."

Raouti turned toward the small warrior with only one eye—lost to Bameeta as a young boy. "Yes, Camo."

How far is it to the big island called Venezuela?"

"Our old warriors say it is the same distance as it is from our home on Martinique to Zeteena's Island."

"Ah, it is not so far as I thought."

"But," Raouti stopped talking and looked at his other chiefs, to be certain that they were listening. "It is across a treacherous channel to Trinidad, where the giant named

Baracoraima lives. He has many warriors, and even though they are not trained fighting men such as we are, they are many. We must be very watchful, so that a large war fleet of Arawak warriors do not catch us dreaming about the young girls we will capture on the way home."

"Cacique Raouti."

Raouti turned to the tall thin boy, who was as dark as his mother; a Maroon—<u>Escaped black slave</u>.

"Yes Tano-malu." Raouti and the black boy had grown up together, and remain good friends throughout their long lives.

"How many will go to Trinidad with you?"

"Only one other canoe will go with me, and my sister Bameeta will be in charge of it. She is the best scout in our village and can almost be touching the enemy without him knowing it," he turned to her and smiled, "until she slips the strangling vine around his neck."

Not a sign of emotion showed on the young girl's beautiful, but cruel and expressionless face, however inside she was very excited to be given her first command.

"You will not," he continued, "take any canoes from the Arawak and you will not kill any of them while you are on the big island of Venezuela. Wait until you have gathered all the information that Cacique Ahameke needs. When you begin burning the villages and the canoes they are building, you must then be certain that there are no survivors to carry news of our presence to other Arawak villages before we all have departed and are heading home. Ahameke will expect to see new faces when we arrive, so we will take a few of their canoes and fill them with young girls as we strike the Arawak on the small islands during our trip home. We must put two strong Carib warriors in each canoe with them to see that they paddle hard"

"We will," Tano-malu said smiling, "and each of the girls will already have a baby in her belly."

Raouti smiled back. "Ah yes, my little black Maroon, you most certainly are your father's son." Raouti smiled as his men laughed. All knew about the boy's father, who could be with ten women in one night.

"And never forget," Raouti added, "that we are to bring Cacique Ahameke information, so remember what you see, and be alert so that you are not captured. Ahameke will use the information that we take home with us to prepare a war fleet that will return, and it is then that all of you can kill Arawak until your arm tires from the weight of your war club."

Shortly after dark, Raouti's ten war canoes departed Ronde, the tiny island a mile north of Grenada, and headed south into a calm sea. By dawn they had covered most of the one-hundred-miles to Trinidad. Several questions by his men went unanswered, and Camo finally noticed how intently Raouti was watching the sky. When he turned from looking at the sky himself, the one-eyed boy thought, *clouds in the north are turning dark, and the wind is stronger. I took this calm as a good omen, but I think I was wrong. I know Raouti was watching the sky all night—he misses nothing.*

One hour after the sun rose above the horizon, a strong wind began blowing from the northwest, and was coming through the Lesser Antilles—straight at Raouti's fleet of small canoes. "Check to be certain that all of the calabash dippers are secure." Raouti yelled at his men, and hoped that his other chiefs were instructing their men also. "Some of us will be in the water before we reach the big island." He let the steering oar that was attached to his wrist trail the canoe as he checked the honeysuckle vine that secured the bailing cups made from gourds. He also checked to be certain that his spare steering oar was also secure, and then yelled for his men to check their spare paddles and bailing gourds.

They had cut the distance to land in half when the first dugout capsized. It happened only one hundred yards ahead of Raouti. A land-dwelling Indian could not believe how fast these excellent swimmers had bailed out their canoe, while treading water beside it in the high waves. Before Raouti and his crew of seven came to it, the eight warriors were back inside, with one energetically bailing with both hands, while the rest paddled furiously to regain their position in the fleet.

The twenty-knot wind had grown to gale-force by the time they spotted Venezuela—dead ahead. Every one of the canoes but two had capsized once, and two that were poorly built had dumped its human cargo into the water several times. Months earlier, Raouti and his chosen crew built their own canoe, and he supervised the hollowing out of the one that his sister Bameeta would soon be in charge of—neither had capsized.

When they reached the shallow waters of the coast, he motioned with his steering oar. The plan had been to enter Dragon's Mouth Channel, which ran between Punta Penas and Trinidad, then camp somewhere along the inside shore of Peninsula de Paria, a thin finger protruding into the Caribbean Sea. A change of plans was now needed, so each warrior released the war club from his ankle, where he tied it before beginning each passage. The club was built from dense ironwood and would not float. Each had many sharks' teeth and sharp stones imbedded into the edges.

Not knowing whether or not a traveling group of Arawak warriors had observed them, Raouti wanted to be ready for a fight the moment their dugouts touched the beach.

Luckily there were no nearby Arawak villages, and a short time after landing, all evidence of their arrival had been skillfully removed—under Bameeta's keen eyes.

"Guabancex has given us a sign." Raouti looked to the north, from where the wind was blowing—now at near hurricane force. "We will not go through Dragon's Mouth Channel. She has sent us here for a reason, and here is where you will hunt for Arawak villages to gather the information needed by Ahameke. In this many days," he held up all five digits of each hand, "you will head toward Grenada, where we will all gather again to begin raiding our way home. Bameeta, myself, and the warriors who have been selected to go to Trinidad with us, will wait here as we watch the weather."

Later that night, Raouti instructed all of the warriors to sleep after eating. An hour before dawn he gathered them to him in the dense jungle. "The wind is dropping, so my plan has changed again. Bameeta and I will soon be able to get across Dragon's Mouth Channel to Trinidad."

The warriors chosen to go with Raouti and his sister cast all personal thoughts from their minds, and concentrated intently on their task. Raouti would later tell the war council in Cacique Ahameke's village, as they sat around the fire, "At times our canoes were more out of the water than in, because of the way my men and Bameeta's men were using their paddles."

Raouti was silent for a few moments as he scanned the dark skies, "On our homeward trip we will take Arawak women from Grenada and more from small villages on St Lucia." The young chief grinned, "The Arawak canoes are not as good as ours, but Bameeta and I will each take one with us when we leave Trinidad, and the other warriors will take six when they leave the big island to join us on Grenada." He turned to his sister. "Bameeta, you and your warriors will sleep three hours and then you must all be ready to leave for Trinidad to search for Arawak villages. You and your warriors will cross near us, and I will signal where you should hide your canoe until it is dark to begin searching from there to the north. That is where I will begin searching to the farthest northern tip. Paddle farther north each night and stop when you see their campfires. If you must move again, stop before it is light to hide the canoes again and rest. When the dark has turned to light this many times," once again he held up all five digits of each hand, "you will be almost to the place where I began, so gather your warriors and begin the trip to Grenada where we will meet." He abruptly turned to his own crew and began planning the trip across Dragon's Mouth Channel to the island of Trinidad.

With each of his men paddling, as Raouti steered one canoe and his sister the other, both dugouts made the trip from Peninsula de Paria at the tip of Venezuela to the southern area of Trinidad in four hours. There was no way that Raouti could have known it, but the two canoes had crossed over the same area where his brother, Bapatou, had died at the hands of Baracoraima.

Dragon's Mouth Channel is twenty miles of water so notoriously treacherous that most European sea captains avoid it by going all the way around the tip of the small island of Tobago and enter the Caribbean Sea in the wide water between there and Grenada.

These incredible seafaring Caribbean natives always took the shortest route to their destination, so to them it was always simply a trip directly from where they were to where they wanted to be.

Before leaving for Trinidad, Raouti noticed Bameeta walking toward the area where warriors stood who would take first guard duty. She stood quietly talking to the sentries as he approached and spoke softly to her. "Come sister, you are now in command of warriors." Without a word, he turned and led her and several others toward a clearing, which had been prepared earlier. Bameeta was thrilled with her first command, but remained stoic and silent as she followed her brother and the other warriors.

"My supply chief, Dahani, has given each warrior one small piece of dried fish and each canoe has one large gourd of water for the group to share. We will all receive the same until we are able to replenish our supplies." He looked again at the sky, and saw no stars or slice of moon. "We do not know how long this storm will last, but while it blows loud, our warriors must go through the jungle to find villages to spy on, and gather the information that Cacique Ahameke waits anxiously for." Raouti looked directly at each warrior before once again adding, "We must not fail our cacique."

Bameeta kept her dugout close enough to her brother's dugout to see him raise his hand in the darkness and signal her to land the canoe. With her paddle she tapped the paddler closest to her lightly on the shoulder and motioned toward shore. He did the same and the signal was silently passed to each paddler.

Within the hour, their canoe was carefully hidden and all trace of movement across the beach had been brushed away.

A short time later she watched as Guanikeyu, her best climber and also a fearless warrior, climbed down from a tall palm. He spoke so quietly that others did not hear him tell his cacique that he had seen a small fire not far away. They were soon heading toward their first Arawak village on Trinidad to gather information for Ahameke. They carefully observed every aspect of the village. Bameeta memorized each detail, and then they returned to the hidden canoe and rested during the daytime hours. From here they would put the canoe back in the water each evening, after darkness had covered their movement. After brushing out their tracks they paddled north several miles to begin searching for another village.

When Bameeta cut the tenth notch in her time-stick she gathered her small group together. "Tonight is our last night on this island. We will watch the Arawak until they have gone to the sleeping hammocks, and then we attack. After everyone has been killed we will set fire to all of their small boats but one, which we will take with us to carry what food and supplies they have, and also to carry the women we take from Grenada to our village. If they are also building large canoes like the others we watched, then we must set them all on fire before leaving."

An hour after the sun went down, two warriors were left to guard the canoes, as the others stealthily approached the glowing fires in the distance. Not one word was spoken as they lay watching the enemy, still working beneath torches, on three huge war canoes. They used tools similar to those that the Caribs had seen men using in the other Arawak villages. When the Arawak became tired and had gone to their hammocks, Bameeta smiled in the darkness. *Fools! You leave no warriors to guard the village as you take your beer and women to the sleeping place.*

Two hours later, each Carib warrior rose at the sound of a clicking signal, which came from her lips. Their moves had been practiced many times in previous months.

With eyes accustomed to the darkness, they descended upon the sleeping village. Bameeta raised her war club and struck the first lethal blows. The three young children who were sleeping on the ground died without fully awakening. One child's cry caused her mother to partially rise from her hammock, only to feel Bameeta's war club striking her face—repeatedly. As other children were rising sleepily from the ground nearby or from hammocks, Bameeta moved swiftly, dispatching each with blows from her ironwood war club.

"There were no other fires to be seen," Bameeta said after she was certain that all of the Arawak had been slaughtered, "so this must be the only village on this side of the island." She pointed to a group of children, who she had slain earlier, "We will set fire to these huge canoes they have been building, and then roast those Arawak piglets over the coals. When their people arrive from other villages, they will know who has visited them."

By dawn, the burned and mutilated bodies of the adults lay among ashes of the canoes, and the severed remains of several Arawak children. They were purposely strewn about the area where the canoes were burned. With a wave of her arm, Bameeta laughed, "There was not even one Arawak warrior in this village who was brave enough to be consumed by us."

"Yes," a nearby warrior said while holding a tiny cooked foot. "If I cannot have a brave warrior's flesh so that his soul will enter me, then I would rather have this tender Arawak piglet's foot." He gripped the heel with his teeth and tore the charred meat off, and then began chewing. He stopped momentarily to say, "One less Arawak warrior to do battle with in the future."

They carried enough of the cooked children for the canoe guards to consume, and then they were on their way toward Grenada.

Raouti and his men had furiously paddled north until two hours before dawn. The canoes were then pulled into the jungle and concealed. They remained hidden until dark as all rested from their long journey, and then moved along the coast until they spotted a small natural harbor. They arrived an hour before dawn, and worked silently but swiftly to have their canoe hidden in the Trinidadian jungle, and all traces of their arrival on the enemy's island removed. Raouti stood the first guard as all of his exhausted warriors slept. Two warriors awakened at noon and relieved Raouti so he could sleep.

With darkness covering all of their movements, the Carib warriors moved toward a small fire, spotted inland from where their canoes were hidden. For three hours they stealthily approached the Arawak camp, until they lay hidden in the dense brush just beyond the clearing where work on the huge war canoes progressed during the day. *Foolish Arawak,* Raouti thought as he watched, *they post no guards to see us or the fires burning all of their new canoes. We will easily kill them all as we work our way north to the last village before we head to Grenada.*

Raouti's Carib warriors had already been given their orders to slaughter the Arawak villagers as they headed north toward the departure point. They now lay silently watching the village with all of the Arawak warriors in their hammocks asleep.

They attacked with a vengeance, and ten minutes later the campfire was casting light on a ghastly scene. Five Arawak warriors, eleven women, and nine children were dead. Raouti's men ransacked the camp, and after eating everything that was simmering in the pepperpot, they took all food that the Arawak had stored. After administering a final blow to each victim, to be certain that no word could be carried to other Arawak camps. Hearts were cut out and body parts severed to be taken with them...and thrown to sharks. The Arawak would think that a very large band of Carib warriors had devoured their friends and family.

It was important that the Arawak know that the Caribs had paid them a visited. Raouti and his men returned quickly to their canoe and headed north several miles toward a fire spotted earlier.

They were on their way home—blood would flow.

Their journey, from the center of the island to the area where Bameeta would stop after working her way north, had begun. The routine they established on that first night was repeated many times before they headed north and into the Caribbean Sea. Raouti's destination was back toward the meeting with Bameeta and her warriors on the island of Grenada, and then home—with stops along the way to gather women to carry home and breed with.

Raouti's other warriors had moved swiftly along the coast of Venezuela at night, pausing often so their best climber could go to the top of a tall tree to look for a campfire's light coming from an Arawak village. When one was spotted, they quickly pulled their canoes across the beach. With them hidden and all signs of movement across the sand removed, they headed into the jungle in search of the village. Night after night they moved close enough to each, so that they could observe the enemy's movements, and commit to memory all they had seen. What was seen on that first night was repeated in each large camp they silently observed.

. . .

Raouti looked at his time-stick and realized that the notch he just cut in it was the tenth one. He turned to his men, who had been resting all day. "Tonight is our last night on this Arawak island. We will wipe out the village that Camo spotted from the tall gommier tree when they started their evening fire. We will then begin the trip to Grenada to meet with our other warriors."

With darkness covering their movement, they silently headed toward the small village. They lay hidden as five young Arawak men worked on a huge canoe beneath the light from several torches. Two hours after the sun dropped back into the sea to rest, the men removed the torches from their holders and headed toward the nearby camp. They were met by an old woman standing next to the pepperpot holding a gourd scoop. Each man grabbed a gourd bowl to receive hot stew, and then moved toward a flat log resting on two short upright poles. Cassava bread was brought to them by a young girl as another brought beer.

Raouti and his men silently watched until everyone had climbed into their sleeping hammock. One hour later, when they felt certain that all of the exhausted Arawak were asleep, they attacked. The five men were the first to be bludgeoned and then they swiftly slaughtered eight small children, and took nine women captive. One by one each warrior was checked to be certain that all were dead, and then the Carib warriors ate what was left in the simmering pepperpot. After cutting down two vine hammocks, they piled all of the cassava bread and dried fish into one, and the shiny new tools they had seen the men working inside a canoe with, into the other. On top of the tools they put everything they could use on the return trip home to St Vincent. As two men set fire to the two completed canoes and the new one under construction, the others severed limbs from the children and tossed them into a third hammock that Raouti cut down. "We will take these and toss them to sharks, but the Arawak who come to this village will know who has paid them a visit."

"Yes," a warrior said, "they were kind to make so much bread and smoke so many fish, so we do not have to eat their stinky babies." Everyone laughed as they loaded the booty into one of the small Arawak canoes and positioned the nine captives, whose hands they had tied together, around the prize canoe to pull it. They headed back toward the beach and their own canoe.

Raouti timed his departure from Trinidad to bring them close to Grenada before the sliver of moon rose in the sky. Even before the prow of his canoe touched the sand on Point Salinese, he spotted the faint signs of a fire. With his toes gripping the gunwale, Raouti held tight to the steering paddle, which was shoved against the bottom of the canoe, and stretched. *I see fire a long distance from the nearest Arawak camp that I know of. Perhaps the Arawak here are burning out the center of gommier trees to make war canoes? Or could it be the men who wear shiny clothes?*

Raouti directed his paddlers to move quietly to the other canoes. "I see small fires in the distance, so we must go to the beach very silently and conceal our canoes. Two of you will remain on the beach and look for Bameeta and her warriors, and two more must find our other warriors, who I'm certain must have already landed, because they have the fastest canoes. The rest must remain to watch our captive women, as I go to the fire and observe what the people with the fires are doing."

Half an hour later Raouti's warriors had the canoes pulled into the dense brush and their tracks on the beach covered. No sooner had they finished their task than Bameeta stepped silently from the jungle. She whispered as her brother listened intently. "My warriors are so heated about capturing new maidens that they paddled like never before and we landed here long before you and the others." Raouti smiled in the darkness then turned and disappeared once again.

Raouti informed the two warriors who were to search the darkness for Bameeta, that she had already arrived, and to remain with those guarding the captives, and then he left camp alone to see who had fires burning less than a mile away. Within the hour he returned and searched until he located his childhood Maroon friend, Tano-malu.

The black warrior's mother was an African slave taken during a Carib raid against a large group of Spaniards who had established a small settlement on Barbados. She had insisted that he continue to use his native African language while with her, and the Carib language while with his father, the Carib warrior who she married. "You will one day use our language to defeat the white men in shiny clothes. That is why I am also teaching it to your father."

On the night of Raouti's rendezvous on Grenada with his other warriors, and Bameeta and her warriors, Raouti sat in his hidden jungle camp. He said nothing about what he had seen when he had approached the distant fire, because he was considering what the best course of action would be. He listened intently as his men spoke about what they had seen in the Arawak camps on Venezuela. "They were busy preparing a war fleet such as no man has ever seen," one said. And another commented, "I feel certain that we have only destroyed a small part of it."

"Yes!" Another warrior confirmed, shaking his head, "Tunpa—<u>Tree God</u>—must be making the giant gommier trees lie down so that the Arawak can build many canoes and come to our home and conquer us." His brow creased as he frowned, and his eyelids lowered, "They are all using strange tools that make the wood chips fly like birds from the fallen trees. They will soon have many more to replace those we burned. Ogoun has given the Arawak magic. We must not fail in our mission to take this information to Cacique Ahameke."

Raouti was silent a moment then also shook his head. "Yes! It is the only answer. Tunpa has given the Arawak the many carob trees for food and rattles to make music, and the gommier tree to make war canoes. Our Carib ancestors must have angered Ogoun and Tunpa, for the Arawak to receive so many large trees and magic tools to make their war canoes so quickly."

"Every warrior in their villages will soon be working on more giant war canoes to take the place of the ones we destroyed." The Carib who spoke looked up at the sky as though the gods would answer. "I fear we will never again be able to sneak into their canoe building camps after this raid."

"Yes, they will have many guards in trees to spot us long before we are near their villages," another man said. "In one village there were this many being built." He held up both of his hands, and after extending all ten digits, he folded one thumb back across his palm." After lowering his hands, he then held up one and extended all five digits, "And there were this many large war canoes already finished and in a canal nearby. Our fire destroyed some, but there were many Arawak who ran into the forest, so they must have returned and saved some." He shook his head and looked into the small fire, "Those in the canal are ready to carry the Arawak warriors to make war with the Carib Nation."

Orocobix was one of Raouti's most trusted warriors, and a young man not given to exaggeration or undue alarm. Raouti narrowed his already severely slanted eyes, and shook his head as he grunted, "Ummph" through pinched lips.

"There were also some white men," Orocobix continued, "and all of them were either working on the canoes or instructing the Arawak how to use tools such as I had never seen until we attacked the first village."

"The mighty fox-god, Tunpa must be helping them hollow out the gommier trees, because men cannot do so many at one time." The young man who had spoken turned to Raouti, "What must Ahameke do if every Arawak village has been given so many gommier trees by Tunpa?"

Raouti remained silent for a long time before speaking again. "We must be very careful not to be caught, so we can take Ahameke this news about the gods and white men helping the enemy with magic tools."

. . .

After listening as Raouti explained about a very large group of blacks he had seen near the fire, which had been spotted when they first arrived, Tano-malu spoke. "There are many different tribes in my homeland, but the language spoken in some areas is similar enough to be understood by many. I believe I can make them understand that we are friendly and can help them."

Camo moved next to Raouti and spoke quietly to his chief and friend. "Bameeta also spotted the fire before she arrived. She went into the jungle alone and lay next to the blacks to listen, but they speak in a tongue she has never heard. She told me her warriors brought many Arawak paddles from the villages she raided, and can be used by them if you decide to take some of the blacks with us."

Raouti smiled as he thought, *she is not only courageous to go in there alone, but is always thinking ahead.* "Tell her that we also brought extra paddles and we will offer to take some of the blacks with us and return for the rest"

Raouti lay silently in the thick brush and watched as Tano-malu approached the huge gathering of strange blacks. *He is a courageous warrior to go among these strangers alone.*

The blacks watched in awe as the small black native approached alone into the mass of black strangers. Tano-malu continuously used phrases in a variety of African dialects taught to him by his mother. He breathed a sigh of relief when a very large black man smiled and repeated the word *friend* in one of the common dialects.

Raouti silently lay in the jungle and watched for two hours as Tano-malu used hand signs and a variety of words that were alien to the young Carib's ears. He smiled when several of the blacks pressed forward to shake the black hand of his young friend. Tano-malu then turned and headed toward the beach, which was a quarter mile away...in the opposite direction of where his friend lay hidden. Raouti thought, *he is leaving their camp in the opposite direction of where our warriors are. Tano-malu is smart and will be a great cacique one day.*

Raouti and Tano-malu approached Bameeta and her men, plus the others who were a mile away. Raouti touched his sister's arm, and then the arm of each warrior in charge of a canoe. He pointed at an extremely tall palm tree silhouetted against the sliver of moon, now higher in the dark sky. They all headed toward the palm, and when he arrived with the final warrior he spoke quietly. "Tano-malu and I scouted the fire I saw in the distance."

Many were embarrassed that they had not seen a thing in the darkness, as had their cacique and her brother. "There are many African blacks gathered together. They were in chains on a large canoe like the white men use, and the men who wear the shiny clothes became crazy and crashed upon the rocks near the shore. Many drowned but the men that Tano-malu talked with had already learned how to open the chains, and once they were free they opened the chains of others and together they made it to the beach. When the white men who survived the wreck came ashore they killed them all. Tano-malu walked among them alone and learned that it all happened yesterday and they are now frightened that they will be captured and made slaves anyway. Tano-malu told them that we will take as many with us as possible and that if they will not burn a fire and eat only berries, grubs, and bugs until we return to get the rest, they will be allowed to live among us." He paused to observe the reaction of each man.

The young Carib warrior who usually questioned every word that was said, asked, "How many are they?"

"More than one hundred and many are old enough to be warriors and many are women old enough to have babies."

The man paused to think about what he had just learned, and then spoke again. "The black men are fierce fighters, but if they remain here, the blacks are correct; they will be captured by white men again or the Arawak to be used as slaves."

"I have invited them to come and live among us and fight the evil white men." Raouti remained silent as he scanned the eyes of his men, and when he spoke again, it was with authority as their cacique. "These Africans will make our villages stronger, and we will need great numbers to defeat the Arawak and the many white men who are coming, which our old medicine man has seen in his dreams. He told my father to prepare for battles with white men who will come in giant canoes and be everywhere, like the mosquitoes."

The young warrior paused again and looked intently into Raouti's eyes before speaking. "You have done a good thing, my cacique. We need greater numbers if we are to defeat the Arawak and also the men in shiny clothes." He paused a moment while thinking about the terrified black people, "and no person should ever be another man's slave."

Raouti called a messenger to him and spoke quietly. "Tell each war chief that we will rest until the moon is there." He pointed to the spot in the sky where he knew the sliver of moon would be in three hours. "Tell them that we will gather as many of the Africans as we can safely carry and then we must all go out to sea beyond all eyes, so that we can continue paddling unseen until we are home."

Raouti paused a moment before speaking. "On this trip we have seen none of the big canoes of the white men, so Yayjaba is keeping them away from The People, but we must move swiftly if we are to save these blacks." He knew that it would only be a matter of time before the Spaniards or other Europeans arrived to discover the Africans and imprison them until they could be sent to other forts and settlements to once again be enslaved.

Raouti and Tano-malu returned to the African's camp with five men carrying as much food and water-filled gourds as they dared share. The starving people waited patiently as the sparse food was passed to each, and after eating, they again showed great restraint as the gourds with water were passed from one to the other. Tano-malu waited until all were fed and had their thirst temporarily quenched, before speaking in a dialect that they seemed to understand the most words. "If you stay here very long the white men will come and make slaves of you. We can carry some of you to our home, which is three days paddling from here." He pointed in the direction of where they had come from, not where their village was; which was actually one hard twenty-four hours of non-stop paddling—routine for a Carib war canoe. (he was taught as a child to lie about direction and distance to his village) "And then we will return in larger canoes to get the rest of you." He waited while their leaders talked quietly amongst themselves. The very large, very black man he had spoken too earlier moved toward Tano-malu. He smiled as he repeated the word he had earlier understood— *friend.* Tano-malu shook his head up and down and told the large African that he must choose those to go and to tell the rest to quietly wait for them to return for the rest.

None of the Carib warriors but the caciques were told about the Africans, but when a mixed group of thirty young black men and women followed Raouti into camp, his warriors quietly began passing out food and water to them from their supplies.

Each of the large Arawak villages that Raouti's re-con warriors had stealthily approached on Venezuela had the same large dugout canoe building operation. It was a very perplexed group of Carib Indians who departed the island of Grenada with the Arawak dugouts they had taken as war booty, carrying Africans and captive Arawak women, as they headed home toward Martinique.

Behind them they left sixty-one totally destroyed sixty-foot-long war canoes and a dozen that would require a great deal of effort to be reworked into smaller ones. Raouti's mission was far more successful than he would know until many years later.

The sun began rising once again from her sleep beneath the sea, to find all of the Carib war canoes, and the smaller Arawak dugouts; already twenty miles from shore and filled with Caribs and Africans. They turned and began paddling steadily on a northerly heading.

All Carib caciques are well trained to unquestioningly follow the orders given by whoever has been placed in command by their head cacique—in this case their cacique, Ahameke's son, Raouti.

The sharp prows of the small Carib dugouts sliced through choppy seas toward Ahameke's stronghold on the distant island of Martinique—two hundred miles away. Raouti constantly watched the sky and steered the lead canoe. His eyes could spot a lone seagull snatching lunch from a school of glass minnows a mile away. He was continuously searching the horizon for any sign of the large canoes used by the Spaniards, or the smaller war-dugouts of his enemy, the Arawak. *We must quickly tell Ahameke about the Africans, so he can send a large fleet of big canoes to bring them to our village.* He sat in the stern and pulled hard with his steering oar and stopped only long enough, during daylight, to correct their heading by observing the amount of green reflected by the sun from the trees on distant islands they were passing.

Less than twenty-four hours later, Raouti's small band of guerrilla reconnaissance warriors were on a small river on the island of Martinique, and paddling toward Ahameke's village.

Two hours after Raouti had entered the river, Ahameke sat silently listening to his son, as the women of his tribe prepared cassava bread, iguana cooked in coconut oil, and sweet potatoes. The Africans and the Carib warriors had been long without a good hot meal.

Ahameke spoke quietly to Raouti. "You did very well, my son. We need extra warriors now more than ever before, and also many women to create warriors for the future." He then turned to Bameeta, who for the first time was sitting at the Council of Caciques. "Daughter, you did no less than I was certain you would. With the information you and your brother have returned with, we will soon deliver a blow to the Arawak that will forever prevent them from becoming a powerful nation." He then turned to a young Carib warrior who was recently promoted to cacique of a tribe on the eastern end of the island, whose chief had died after being bitten by a fer-de-lance viper. "Go now in six large canoes and bring the rest of the Africans here. Take six small canoes crewed with powerful warriors to lead the way and also to guard your rear in case you meet an enemy." Ahameke looked intently into the young cacique's eyes a moment before continuing, "We want to save these black people from being used as slaves by the evil white men who come in giant canoes, but we also need them very much to help increase our numbers. Use great caution."

The large black African had been watching the small bronze men who were talking. He recognized the word African because his captors had called him and his people by that same word. Since it was what these men also called him and his tribe, he understood that the word African was not a slur or bad word...it was simply what they were. When Ahameke motioned with his arm in the direction that the Africans had just came from, he sensed that orders were given for canoes to be sent to bring them to this new camp. Unknown to the Carib, he was the chief of a group who had been captured and chained aboard the doomed slave vessel. The huge black man was also a very courageous and brazen warrior in his home land. He now approached the group and looked directly at Ahameke when he spoke. "Friend," he said as he touched his broad chest and then pointed in the direction where he had determined the rest of his people were waiting. He pantomimed paddling and touched his chest again before pointing in the direction of Grenada.

Ahameke silently watched the huge black man as he attempted to communicate with him. He told Raouti to summon Tano-malu, and then shook his head slowly up and down at the African, who immediately smiled and repeated the word friend twice in the Carib language.

When Tano-malu arrived moments later, Ahameke then instructed the youth to ask the African if he was the chief of the blacks. After a series of attempts at words in the African dialects he knew, and several hand signs, Tano-malu turned to Ahameke. "Yes, my cacique, he is the chief of some but not all, however they will all obey his orders because their chiefs were all killed."

"Tell him that he can go with my warriors and get the rest of his people, and we will make offerings to Adamisil Wedo, to protect them until they return."

The African understood enough to know that he was being allowed to accompany the bronze men. He smiled wide again, revealing a mouth full of perfect white teeth, and once again touched his chest while repeating the words good man in his tongue. Tano-malu smiled and shook his head; saying "iroponti quekelli," while pointing at the African. The black chief was pleased that he had communicated with his rescuers.

Bameeta had been watching the naked African the entire time since she and the others had arrived with him on her island. She had never seen a more perfectly formed man, from his broad shoulders all the way down to his muscular legs, including the huge penis hanging between them. She had spent time in the bushes with a few young Caribs, and had been separated from her virginity, but had never experienced orgasm, consequently had not been impressed by the experience. Those events had however, opened the way for her desires, and she now felt a rush of hormones running through her ripe young body as she turned to her father. "I will return with them in one of the small canoes to be certain that no harm comes to our warriors or the Africans."

Ahameke missed nothing when he gathered his caciques around a council fire. He exercised great subtlety as he carefully observed the body language and speech inflections of each of his caciques. These two observations provided him with great insight to the true events being described by warriors, who often embellished a story to cast a better light upon their involvement. He had earlier noticed his daughter often watching the huge black African with intense interest, and he approved. *The children she will have with that man will be a great asset to this village.* He nodded his head at Bameeta, and then stood and headed toward the simmering pepperpot to see what had been added since he last ate a gourdful.

All of the remaining Africans were picked up without incident and easily brought to Ahameke's camp. Bameeta accompanied the huge African as he explained in the most common dialect in the African language what they could expect from their rescuers, and also what would be expected of them. Bameeta asked Tano-malu to stay with them until all of the still-terrified Africans understood as much as was possible, under the circumstances that cast them into Carib society, what their future would be like.

The young Maroon quickly picked up the many various dialects that were now circulating among the Africans, and before a fortnight had passed he was able to communicate easily with any group.

Bameeta asked Tano-malu to help her learn the language of the huge African. The huge black had been unanimously elected by the Africans themselves, to serve as the chief of all Africans, and Bameeta wanted to be able to better communicate with him and the others. When she didn't understand something that was said, she stopped Tano-malu and had him explain what was said and how she should say it. In this way, Bameeta was quickly building a large vocabulary of African words, which made communicating easier with the huge man that she had already decided was soon going to be her husband. Her knowledge of a variety of African dialects would serve her and the Caribs greatly in the years of turmoil and battle that lie just beyond the horizon.

Bameeta approached her father and asked if he would sit and talk to her about something she felt was important to the Carib Nation. He nodded toward the shade of a large tree, and headed toward it with her following.

"I have already noticed the lines of deep thought crossing your brow. What is bothering you, daughter?"

She began immediately and looked directly into his eyes as she spoke; a trait that he admired in her since she was a child. "We have five different languages being spoken by the Africans, because the slavers took them from different areas of their homeland. When the slightest problem arises, it takes a very long time to get everything worked out, and the people settled down once again and working on things that will make their lives and our village better."

When Ahameke remained silent while staring into her eyes, Bameeta continued. "I believe that all of the Africans and our people too, will benefit if we begin teaching the Africans to speak and also to understand our language." Without waiting, Bameeta began laying out her plan to accomplish it. "Tano-malu has now mastered all five of their dialects, and told me that he would enjoy helping them learn how to speak our language." She grinned and added, "There are several young maidens that have caught his eye, and he wants to spend more time among them." She replaced the grin with a serious set to her face and continued, "it will never work if we allow the Africans to try to learn only when they feel like it, and not when they don't. They are a very hard working people and could build a large cover to keep the sun from causing them to become tired and distracted. With no walls it would be a very cool area with the ocean breeze running through, and they would learn more quickly."

Ahameke yelled for a passing young warrior to bring him and his War Cacique a gourdful of cassava beer. Bameeta felt honored to be called War Cacique, rather than daughter, and after they each took a long refreshing drink, he nodded agreement. "You have obviously been thinking about this a long time and have solved a problem for our people. I have not been able to convey my wishes to these people and help them understand that we want them to live among us as equals and not slaves."

"Yes, father. When they can hear your words and understand what is said, then they will be a much happier people and we will all benefit. One thing you must do though, is to make a decree; that it is required of all Africans to attend every time that Tano-malu calls them to the speak house.

During the following week, many of the Africans joyfully arrived each day to work on the structure under which they would learn to speak the language of their rescuers.

As the long hot months passed, Ahameke found himself communicating more easily with the people that had been saved from a fate far worse than death. He listened intently as they told him about the treatment they had suffered at the hands of the Portuguese slave traders. Repeatedly he listened to stories of senseless abuse of the men and boys, and of the repeated raping of women, very young girls, and a few of the young boys too.

The huge black that Bameeta had chosen as her husband, learned the Carib language quickly and he and Ahameke conversed often. "I believe," Ahameke once said, "that the men who stole you and these Africans are the same men that we have seen searching our islands. We did not then know what they were looking for, but it is now very certain that it was people they wanted." A deep scowl crossed his bronze face as he scanned the jungle surrounding his camp. "I will send more scouts out to observe the area between here and the only calm water where the men who wear shiny clothes can bring their huge canoes in from the sea. When they arrive, and I am sure they will, because we see their canoes passing far out near the edge where the water drops off, they will find what they search for." He turned toward the man who would eventually be named Gauban, and a wide grin spread across his face as he spoke. "They will find more men than they hoped for, and you and your people will have your revenge."

The shelter that was named the Speak House soon became a social gathering for not only the Africans, but many of the Caribs as well. When the Africans began understanding the language, under the tutelage of the bright little Maroon, many Carib women and a few older men, began arriving to mingle among them during their frequent breaks. "These people," a middle-aged Carib woman once commented to Bameeta, "have endured far more than our ancestors did when the men in shiny clothes began killing our people on the big island."

"Yes, Atoanni, their own people assisted the men who came onto their land to steal them, and now they will never see their homeland again." Bameeta looked around, and then continued, "if I was taken to a completely new land where I could not even speak the language, I would feel very lost and would probably die of a broken heart."

"I have thought that too, since they have learned our language and have told me stories about their lives when they lived among their people and friends." Atoanni shook her head slowly while watching the African men talking to

Caribs, and drinking cassava beer in the shade of the speak house. "They are very determined to learn our language and what we eat, and all of the plants we use to make the food taste better."

"Few of them ever complain," Bameeta said, "and then when they do it is always something personal going on among themselves and has nothing to do with us." She grinned at her friend, "I'm sure I would be squawking like a parrot all the time if I was one of them."

"It was very wise of you and your brother to bring them here to live with us."

"It was Raouti who decided to bring them here, and I only agreed with him."

By winter, the Africans were all speaking the Carib language well enough to ask advice about which plants were edible and which were medicinal. They also learned from the Caribs which trees to use for the construction of their homes, and what areas of the shore to send the young boys to search for driftwood. The boys were taught never to all be searching with eyes down, but to always have one set of eyes scanning the entire horizon for the giant canoes of the men in shiny clothes.

The five separate groups of Africans soon had five very large communal houses completed. With help from Carib women, they quickly had enough hammocks woven for sleeping, and relaxing during the day.

Their lives had turned from scenes of horror to a reasonably well-organized existence, which even though it was in a completely new and totally different environment, was more often than not pleasant and relaxing. The bulging bellies of many young African maidens displayed the evidence of contentment, and more than a few of the new crop of babies would have the features of a Carib Indian.

Some of the African men who had been captured along the coast were fishermen, and soon had dozens of traps constructed of material that was similar to what they used in

Africa. Carib men watched and soon began helping. The Carib method of trapping fish was to select an area of river that was near the sea. Then when the tide was high, and sea fish moved into the river as far as they could to feed on smaller fish until it became too fresh, the men placed a long line of stakes, driven into the bottom from one side to the other. As the tide went out they moved farther up the river and sealed it off with another row of stakes. At low tide they entered the sealed off section and launched a few dugouts into the area that held the fish. After spearing the larger ones they wanted, the stakes were removed and laid aside until food was once again needed, and the entire process was repeated. It was very labor intensive, so when they accompanied the Africans on a fishing trip to the nearby reef in a long dugout canoe, they were attentive as the traps were baited with the meat of several conchs.

The reed and stick traps were small rectangular shaped affairs three feet wide and four feet long, with a small opening from top to bottom on each long side. It protruded slightly and the inside wall continued a foot and angled closer to the outer wall, which allowed a slippery fish to swim in to get at the conch meat, which was secured to the bottom in the center of the trap. When the fish decided to leave, he found it impossible. If he was lucky enough to locate the opening where he entered, he could not get past the protruding ends of the pointed sticks.

The traps were baited and set in the shallower waters inside the reef. Ten traps were carried out the first time, and were dropped over as soon as the men could see the bottom to determine where to place each trap.

Buoys were made by selecting aged brown coconuts and then, by using a long thin tool made from a dead Spaniard's knife, an older African man penetrated the soft eye of the hard shell in the center of the coconut husk. It required great skill and patience to locate the eye without removing the husk, but the man performed the feat with ease. Ahameke watched and when he commented how difficult it must be, the man grinned wide and then answered, "Cacique Ahameke, I have done this since I was a very young boy."

Once the milk was drained from each coconut, a concoction made of tree resin and chopped coconut fibers, resembling the oakum used by ship builders to seal their vessel's seams, was shoved into the hole. Three of these enclosed in a woven vine net and attached to the vine rope made a good buoy, and allowed the men to constantly move along the line to pull the traps.

The method of fishing used by the Caribs had very little danger attached. A large moray eel or stingray would occasionally find itself trapped between the stakes, and if aggravated by the natives removing the stakes, would sink its teeth or tail barb into a leg.

Fishing with traps near the reef was another situation altogether. The vine rope was checked each time for wear and if necessary replaced or mended. If a trap filled up with fish, which they often did, then it placed a greater strain on the vine rope. If it snapped in two before the trap could be grabbed, then someone must take a new vine rope, which was always carried in the dugout, and dive down to attach it.

Even prior to setting the traps in the morning, sharks were always cruising along the reef. After pulling them once, the activity of the fish inside, plus the scent of conch meat, always brought several sharks to investigate. Stabbing them with spears usually caused most sharks to leave in search of an easier meal.

Ahameke enjoyed fishing and often went with the men to the reef. While sitting at the fire one evening a short time after it happened, he told Bameeta and Raouti about one incident that he witnessed. "I watched as a trap came toward the surface, and I could see that it was full. One of the Africans reached into the water to grab it by the end, when without warning it suddenly broke free. The man holding the rope was your brother's friend Ahana-mano, and he cursed Olokum for taking our fish back. I told him that it was foolish to blame the Gods, because it was our fault. We should have more carefully checked the vine ropes before leaving. He grunted like a pig and threw the rope to the bottom on the canoe, then picked up the spare rope and said he would dive down and tie it to the trap, and we would have our fish after all. The water was not deep and we could see him very clearly as he tied the vine to the end, but then a large tigershark rushed in and grabbed Ahana-mano right in the middle of his skinny body. It was the biggest tiger that I have ever seen, and with the body in its huge jaws it came straight up and out of the water while shaking its head. It was not a full canoe length from us when it cut him into two pieces, and as we watched, it ate first one and then returned to the bottom and grabbed the other half of Ahana-mano."

The old warrior shook his head, "After the shark incident, the vines were very carefully inspected prior to leaving."

7

~ Raid on the Arawak ~

Ahameke called his daughter Bameeta to a tribal council meeting. "I want you to assemble a war fleet to teach the Arawak a lesson, but first I want you to come to a gathering of our war chiefs."

"Yes father, you are also my cacique and I do as you say."

"Come, they are assembled and waiting."

When Ahameke and Bameeta arrived at the council hut,

every War Cacique stood.

When one by one, each man approached Bameeta and held out his closed fist, she was puzzled. She opened her hand below the offered fist and was again surprised to see a small shell drop into it. Each chief stepped aside to allow another to take his place, and the same thing was repeated until each of them had dropped a shell into her hand. She remained rigid and straight, but Bameeta's confusion was obvious to her father. He had studied her closely during several dangerous and often bloody battles with Arawak, Spaniard, and others—he knew her well. "You have been voted the new cacique of the village on Shell Island. That is where you will choose the warriors to go with you to Trinidad one day soon, and leave Baracoraima, the Arawak who killed my son; your brother Bapatou, a lesson that he shall never forget."

Bameeta was stunned into silence, and could not move for a few moments. There had never been a female Carib Cacique. Regaining her composure, she spoke with a strong voice. "I will make my cacique and his war chief's proud. All Arawak villages will tremble with fear when they hear the name Ahameke. And the giant Arawak, Baracoraima, will wish that he had never brought his people into our islands. I will leave for Shell Island at dawn, and when I arrive I shall prepare my warriors for the journey, and await your orders." She pursed her lips and paused a moment as she looked left and right, until spotting the huge African. She turned back to Ahameke and said, "if you have no objections, I will take the big African with me."

Her father smiled when he spoke. "Yes! He will be a great asset to your new village, and you will never lay in the sleeping hammock alone and cold." She smiled widely and left the hut with her heart still fluttering with great happiness. *I am Cacique Bameeta*, she thought as she went to her small canoe to check it very closely and be certain there were no repairs needed before beginning their arduous one-hundred-mile journey through the chain of small islands, which made up the Windward Islands. *I am now the most powerful woman in the entire Carib Nation.*

After assuring herself that the canoe was ready, she summoned Tano-malu, and then they both went to the huge black African. Even though she knew that he spoke and understood her language very well now, she wanted to be certain he understood that she would be the cacique of a tribe of Caribs on a small island. He smiled at Bameeta and then stood silent as she explained that she wanted him to travel with her to another island where she would become their new chief.

Tano-malu made sure the African understood her completely, and when he finished, the African smiled and nodded his head up and down as he said *I will always be your friend* in the Carib language, while putting a huge forefinger to his broad, bare chest.

Bameeta and the African would arrive on Shell Island two days later, but as the first day of paddling began coming to an end, the African suggested they stop and spend the night on one of the small islands they were passing. He raised the spear he had made soon after being rescued, "I will get us something to eat." He smiled wide, his beautiful white teeth capturing her dark eyes. "It will be nice having you all alone to hold, and no children jumping on my back." Bameeta's eyes shifted to his, and she returned his smile.

"I will hang our sleeping hammock and gather dry wood for a cooking fire, and await your catch."

They agreed on a very small island that had ample trees in which to conceal the dugout in case an enemy vessel was passing near enough to see them. After carrying the small canoe into brush near the water, they dragged it to a large copse of trees a hundred yards from the beach. She told him to go and get something for them to eat, and she would remove their tracks from the sand.

Bameeta removed the long knife from her only item of clothing, a sheath attached to a belt that her brother Raouti had made for her from a tanned wild pig's hide. She cut a branch from a small tree, and once all traces of their arrival was brushed away, she strung the wide, two-person hammock between two trees.

Reaching into the canoe she brought out a small parcel, made of cured wild pig hide, and laid it next to a small area she had cleared of all brush. A few minutes of searching yielded ample wood for a small smokeless fire, on which to cook anything that her man was able to spear. She thought about waiting to see if he was successful, but then decided against it and began to assemble a small fire. *That man will probably bring enough for now and more to carry with us tomorrow.*

Bameeta carefully assembled the dry sticks. First she put down a bed of dry grass, and then added tiny dry twigs that were abundant, instead of using those she carried in the pig hide along with all of her fire making tools. Once she was satisfied that her woodpile was ready, she laid down the piece of ironwood with a shallow indentation in the center. Before placing the one inch thick, round, tapered ironwood spinning rod into the indentation, she settled into as good a position on her knees as possible, to be comfortable while spinning the 15 inch long rod between her hands. Once she began heating the area where the rod and indentation met by spinning the rod, she could not stop and allow it to cool.

With her typical determination to succeed at whatever she attempted, Bameeta began. Starting at the top, she made the rod spin fast by rubbing it between her hands as she slowly allowed them to go down toward the ironwood plate, all the while keeping pressure downward to create friction. When she reached the bottom, she deftly, and with great speed and agility brought her hands back to the top to begin again. After ten minutes she was sweating profusely, but she neither stopped nor slowed her pace. Five minutes later she stopped just long enough to shove the dry grass against the place she was heating, and then more vigorously began spinning the rod again. A minute later she saw smoke, but continued until it was billowing out around the base of the rod. Another two minutes and she let go of the rod and bent closer to blow into the heated area. In seconds a small flame began, and as she blew into it, Bameeta began carefully placing twigs on top.

After building up the fire with increasingly larger twigs, she added four pieces of large dry wood, and then began wrapping her fire making tools in the pig skin, to which she added a little of the dry grass.

She had already seen the stand of banana trees a short distance away, so after severing several fronds, she cut off a small stalk of the tiny wild fruit that grows unattended on many Caribbean islands. Laying the fronds and fruit in their camp, Bameeta used her knife to sever a batch of small green limbs from the nearby trees.

One hour later, the African walked into the camp with one red grouper weighing at least eight pounds, and one hogfish that weighed three. She had completed two criss-cross racks on which to cook the fish that she knew he would bring. "So," he said with a wide white smile, "you had great faith that your man would come home with fresh food."

He had already gutted the fish while near the water, so it only took Bameeta a few minutes to slice along one side of the backbone of each, and then spread them flat on one of the racks, and placed the other rack on top. While she held the two cooking racks together, he wove a long piece of honeysuckle vine around the edges. He held the rack while Bameeta cut three green limbs from a small tree and trimmed them of side branches. Once she had two shoved in the sandy soil at an angle, he placed the grill on them and held it as she placed the third one on the opposite side to keep the weight of the fish from pushing the grill into the coals.

She stood and suggested that they use what daylight remained to see if there was any fruit on the island. He shoved his large frame up by using the long spear, and smiled, "Your islands have many things that I have never eaten and I enjoy them all." After only a few minutes walking, he pointed with his spear, "Are those the bushes that the fruit with many black seeds grows on?"

Bameeta was several inches shorter than him so couldn't see what he was pointing at. "Walk toward them and we will see." Another few minutes and she spotted them. "Ah yes, papaya. I love them too, and look at that tree over there." She pointed toward a head-high tree with round green fruit hanging from its limbs. "Sour fruit to squeeze on the fish we eat here and to help cure the second one as it cooks dry during the night." You get us each a papaya and I will pick as many as I can carry, and in the morning we will put them in the canoe to eat on the trip to Shell Island."

When they returned to the small glowing fire, Bameeta sliced one of the wild sour oranges in half and squeezed it on both fish, and then had him help her turn the grill over. After squeezing a second orange on the cooked side, she carefully placed three short dry limbs of wood on the coals. Before she could bend down to do it, the African was already down and blowing on the coals. She smiled thinking, *this man never needs to be told what to do.*

After they finished eating half of the grouper, which she placed on banana leaves, Bameeta plucked both eyeballs from the head. "I always save this delicious treat for last. Do your people eat the eyes?"

A large white grin spread quickly across his shiny black face. "The eyeball is my favorite part, but I did not want to be greedy and grab them."

"Ha, ha." Bameeta laughed deeply and his smile grew. "I have never met a man who cares even a little bit what his woman wants." She handed him one of the huge crunchy eyeballs, "let us always share what we have."

They silently chewed the delicious tidbit. After slicing off the top of one of the green coconuts he had gathered earlier, he handed it to Bameeta. As she drank the cool refreshing water, which was stored inside awaiting the conversion to begin that would create the coconut meat and milk, the African spoke quietly in a sincere voice, "I will be happy to share the rest of my life with you."

"I will be proud to have you for my man until my life here in the Land of Man ends." She stood and pointed at the sun as it disappeared on the horizon, "The warm sun goes to her rest in the sea again to let us sleep in the coolness of the moon."

The falling sun highlighted her naked body, and it aroused him. He stood, then went to her and moved close as he wrapped his long arms around her from behind, and held her breasts tenderly. She had never been treated tenderly by any of the men and boys she had allowed to have sex with her, and it aroused her greatly. She closed her dark eyes as he brushed his fingertips lightly across her nipples—now becoming swollen and erect.

After several minutes she slowly turned to face him, and looked up into his eyes. He leaned down and locked his lips to hers, as she took his huge erect penis in one hand and began gently caressing his testicles with the other. Reaching around her, he began massaging her buttocks and they both stood silently enjoying the feeling, while emitting sounds of pleasure as they continued kissing.

Without removing his lips from hers, he cupped her tight buttocks and gently lifted her until she could wrap her legs around him and lock her heels to his bulbous muscular buttocks. Bameeta guided his penis into her and then held to his waist as he stood rigid and began moving her body to him and holding it there a brief moment before moving her slowly away until she was at the end of his penis. He slowly repeated the movement over and over...never rushing and never removing his lips from hers.

Bameeta had experienced her first orgasm on the first night she slipped away from camp with the African. She enjoyed the feeling but until this moment on the small island, she had no idea what sexual ecstasy was. The first orgasm she had, while her man held her up as though she was a child, was an experience that she knew few women would ever know. Her female friends talked about their own sexual experiences, and often laughed about the frantic moves the men they were with made. They joked about their men not being able to last long enough for them to also enjoy it.

Expecting to be lowered to the ground when she felt his orgasm, Bameeta was surprised when he continued holding her up, and remained inside of her. He began a dance inside her mouth with his tongue. She had never experienced anything so pleasant and immediately joined him. As their tongues danced, their bodies responded. He became erect again and she felt a rush of hormones, as his tongue dancing around in her mouth with hers, causing her to have shivers rush up and down her entire body, and before long she experienced a second orgasm. It was not explosive and dynamic like the first, but was more intense and lasted longer—much longer. When he held her tight to him and groaned she knew he was also having a second orgasm.

Certain that he was unable to hold her up any longer, she allowed her legs to go limp and release the lock she had on his buttocks. When he slowly raised her up, while still holding her buttocks, to begin running his tongue around her nipples, she realized that he was not finished. Smiling, she knew that she also wanted more of this incredible African.

After both experienced a third orgasm, they turned the rack with the fish over, and then walked to the beach to cool off and cleanse their bodies. Bameeta rubbed his broad back with sand and said, "You are a man that other men must fear when you get near their women."

"I was a man who wanted only the woman who was my African wife." He looked toward the rising moon, "The men who took us to sell as slaves put her with a group to go on another boat, and I know that I will never see her again. Cacique Ahameke explained to me that I must make babies with many Carib girls, and I will, because your people must be multiplied if they are to survive." He took her hand and continued, "Bameeta, I will always be your husband." His bright grin in the moonlight made her feel good. "The first moment that I saw you on the island where we were stranded, there was a glowing light surrounding you, and I knew that we would always be together."

She rinsed the sand from her hands and put her arms around his slender waist, "It is what I want."

Together they walked to their camp, and while Bameeta squeezed limejuice on the fish, he shook the hammock to be certain there were no unwanted scorpions or other visitors to disturb their sleep.

. . .

The greeting they received upon their arrival at Shell Island surprised her. Their sentries, high in the trees had obviously been watching for her, but until she spotted Tano-malu she had no idea how they knew she was coming. When he saw her looking at him, he smiled wide and made motions to imitate frantic paddling. She smiled back and climbed from her small dugout. *He must have left soon after we talked to this African.*

Over fifty young Carib men followed a warrior, much older than her father, as he approached. "Welcome to your new village, Cacique Bameeta." He looked at the huge black man and smiled saying, "Welcome to our island." Tano-malu stood nearby smiling as the African said repeatedly *friend*, while touching his chest. "You will find our warriors strong and courageous," the old Carib said to Bameeta, "and also very anxious to attack the Arawak. We all dream of the day when they are all living with Ghede."

She smiled at the old warrior. "My father told me that G'hana is still a great warrior and will help me plan a raid." She placed both hands on his shoulders, "G'hana, I am honored to be chosen as the new cacique to lead the mighty warriors of Shell Island." She placed her right arm around her father's lifetime friend's withered old shoulders and walked with him to his small wooden house. "You can now spend all of your time growing the good things to eat that my father says you love to do."

"I am already doing that." He looked at her and grinned.

"I am honored to be with a man who my father has always praised as a great warrior. With your council, I will make all of the Arawak that I meet wish their ancestors had remained on the big island and became slaves to the white men who wear shiny clothes."

"And our warriors are honored to have the daughter of the great Ahameke to lead them into battle and victory." He motioned with his hand toward the jungle. "A short distance away, a feast awaits. We knew you would be hungry when you arrived, so we have prepared for it." He smiled again while rubbing his stomach. "There are pigeons, doves, parrots, manatee, turtle, fish, crabs, lobsters, peppers, guava, cor…Bameeta held up her hand while grinning.

"I can listen no longer, G'hana, let us go to the food." To herself she thought, *I wish we had not eaten the other half of that grouper and the papaya on the way here.*

The old warrior put his arm around her slender waist and together they walked toward the feast, alongside the African. The old man turned a smiling face to her, "I too am very hungry, because my wives would not let me eat anything until you arrived."

Bameeta lied, "My man and I did not have time to eat much, so we will enjoy this feast that you and your people prepared; thank you for your kindness."

Tano-malu, who was with then said, "I am having a feast at this very moment." He looked at Bameeta and grinned as he wobbled his eyebrows and nodded toward two young maidens swaying nakedly ahead of them.

She reached out and tussled his short kinky black hair, "I believe many of our new warriors are going to look a lot like you."

"Yes! They will." The young Maroon smiled at Bameeta.

"To give the young warriors who live here a chance, I am soon going to send you home."

"That is a good idea," he smiled saying, "because some of the young men here are beginning to look at me with evil eyes."

"I have already noticed, and do not want to awaken one morning and see your head resting on a pole. Prepare to leave here in three or four days, because I want Cacique Ahameke to know that everything is going very well."

The old man leaned forward and turned toward Tano-malu. "Tell my old friend, Ahameke, that we on Shell Island thank him for sending his daughter to be our new cacique."

After everyone had eaten, the food was left out, with young boys and girls fanning it with palm fronds to keep the bugs away. Young Carib warriors and their maidens came to regularly grab a steamed crab or take a slice of manatee, and then rushed off into the forest to continue making love, and hopefully new babies. As day turned to night, the fire was built up and dancing began.

When the women completed their dance, and the warriors moved into the dancing area, Bameeta was surprised to see her African join them. She smiled as she watched him quickly pick up the beat and rhythm of the Carib men. She was very pleased to see how graceful he moved to the beat of drums. Her dark eyes followed him, and she felt a swelling of passion as his huge penis slapped back and forth against his two muscular thighs. *I will be proud to call this black African warrior my man.*

When everyone tired of dancing they sat at the fire and waited for their old storyteller to arrive. All noise abruptly stopped, and Bameeta intuitively followed the eyes of her new warriors and their ladies. A very old man was shaking two small gourds, whose seeds had been removed and dried before returning them to the cured gourds. He soon appeared in the distant light radiated from the fire...bent with age and moving slowly as he approached.

With no hesitation he began telling one story after another about G'hana's feats as a warrior, and then his wisdom as their Cacique for thirty years. As he spoke, the village maidens carried cassava beer to the warriors and their new Cacique and her black friend. Tano-malu was in the bushes with his second maiden, and did not get any beer or hear the stories. When the old man finished telling stories about G'hana, he began elaborating about the battles that their new Cacique had fought in. Bameeta's mouth dropped open a bit as the old storyteller rambled on, and she was surprised when each story was told basically as it had happened.

As she listened, her life unfolded, from their childhood practice war games when she almost, according to the storyteller, created a girl from a warrior by severing his tiny penis with her toy wooden sword. Everyone laughed and clapped their hands while chanting, *warrior to woman*. The storyteller then told about her battle with two Arawak warriors, who she sent to live with Ghede, by severing one's femoral artery and cutting the other's throat. She wondered, *how does this old storyteller know so much about me?*

A short time later she glanced across the fire, and saw Tano-malu hugging a very pretty Carib maiden—his third. Bameeta smiled very slightly as she thought, *now I know why you paddled so hard to get here before me.* Her smile widened as Tano-malu and the young girl ran into the forest.

During the following weeks, Bameeta and her new tribe became acquainted and very comfortable in one another's company. Tano-malu remained for only three more days, and in that time he told the warriors that were his own age, more about her courage and ferocity in battle. She was immediately accepted by all, due in part to her willingness to participate in everything that advanced her tribe. While smoking a pipe of tobacco, which was grown by the village, with G'hana and several warriors, Bameeta turned to the old warrior. "While the African and I were walking inland yesterday with one of your wives, I saw fresh raised vegetable beds with men working in them. What are you planting, G'hana?"

"Five new gardens," he replied smiling, pleased that she took so much interest in her new village, "are for peanuts, five others for pineapple, and the other five will be for more tobacco." He turned to her and grinned, "Children who sat on my knee only a short time ago it seems, are now warriors who have learned that smoking tobacco is very pleasant."

"In Cacique Ahameke's village also; children grow so fast that all warriors must put as many babies in the bellies of girls as they can, to replace those killed in raids against the Arawak."

"Ah yes," the old Carib warrior said, while a grinning toothless smile spread across his weathered leathery face, "very hard work for our men too, and I fear that time has made me too old to help them."

"G'hana, if one of the maidens on this island went into the bushes with you, I'm sure she would come out with a baby in her belly."

"Hmmmmmm, perhaps!" his head wobbled up and down slowly. "It seems that some parts of a man still work well on the day he goes to the other world."

My father says that there will be many young maidens waiting in the other world for the brave Carib warriors who fought bravely while in the Land of Man. He told me many stories about your raids on the Arawak and strange white men, and he laughed when he said that you caused the maidens to sleep all day, after being in the bushes with you at night."

"I think he was right, but it was so long ago that I am no longer sure it was me." His face looked younger to Bameeta when he grinned and said, "not as often as then, but I am still enjoying my three young wives and look forward to having new babies to hold on my lap and tell stories to." He pointed toward a small mountain in the distance, "Did you walk in that direction yet?"

"No! The African and I followed your wife Nabina to the new raised vegetable beds, and then we went to the old beds where the men were planting cuttings for a new crop of cassava." She raised her hand to shield her eyes against the sun, and looked in the direction he was pointing. "What is over there?"

"My favorite food...come, I will show you." The old man surprised Bameeta by heading toward the area at a brisk jog.

Half a mile later, they came to a clearing full of papaya bushes, and he hadn't changed his pace the entire way, plus he was not breathing hard.

"G'hana, you should not have shown me these, fore I fear that you will no longer have any for yourself." She walked straight to a large bush-like tree and plucked a ripe papaya, pulled out her knife to split it, scooped the seeds into her hand to be dried later, and then bit into the sweet orange meat. "Mmmmmmm, but I am so glad you did." She chewed the sweet ripe fruit with her eyes closed. "These are much sweeter than those we brought from the small island we stopped at."

He smiled, knowing that he brought pleasure to his new cacique. "I have loved the papaya since I was a small boy, but much more now, because my teeth have gone to the other side without me, and the papaya does not make me work hard for something good to fill my old belly." His toothless grin was wide when she opened her eyes. "Come, we are eating land crabs tonight, and I want to be sitting near the boiling pot when they are taken out." He turned and began the same jogging pace as earlier.

Bameeta put the last large chunk of the fruit in her mouth and held the other half as she followed the old warrior, while still chewing. After swallowing it, she turned toward G'hana still marveling at the old warrior's stamina. "I saw the pens where you cleanse the crabs so the meat will be sweet, and there must be five hundred crabs in there."

"Ha!" He laughed while maintaining his pace, "maybe not so many as your hungry eyes counted, but enough to fill the bellies of all who enjoy eating the black crabs."

"We have a very large colony too." Bameeta jogged along with the old warrior, but was finding it difficult to talk, which made her determined to begin running on the sandy beach every morning to build up her stamina and wind. "Cacique Ahameke's oldest wife pens them for several days, and feeds them crushed corn and papaya to make the meat sweet."

The old man turned toward her but kept up his pace, "Papaya! Hmmm, I will tell the women to try that, because they use only crushed corn boiled thick, and sometimes the meat is not sweet." He slowed to a walk as they entered the village, and Bameeta noticed that he was not breathing a bit harder that if he had just walked from one thatched house to another. She was, and thought, *tomorrow I begin running on the beach.*

While Bameeta and G'hana were getting to know each other, The African was busy getting to know the warriors. Even though he could not yet speak their language with ease, he could communicate with the many words he knew, plus his gregarious manner and ability with hand signs, allowed him to communicate with them enough to convey his desire to accompany them and learn about their village. His huge size and friendly attitude helped sway the few who were uncertain about him being an asset to the Carib village, and soon all welcomed him to live among them.

One month after her arrival on Shell Island, Bameeta was surprised to hear the eastern lookout yell, "Canoes coming." She immediately had her warriors put the canoes in the water. She commanded one fleet of ten small canoes, and the African led the other ten.

. . .

Bameeta and her brother Raouti, and their warriors had brought word back to Ahameke about the large canoes being built by Baracoraima on the smaller islands of Grenada, St. Lucia, Trinidad, and the large one, Venezuela. They used the many ancient old gommier trees and irregularities in the coastline as landmarks to pinpoint where the canoes were being built.

Ahameke had been talking with his war chiefs about the information since the day that he received it, and finally decided that it was time to strike a severe blow to the Arawak Nation before they had built enough canoes to replace those burned by Raouti and Bameeta's warriors. Bameeta worried that the Arawak might build a new fleet fast enough with their new tools to strike before Ahameke decided to attack them.

Bameeta and the African were working in the tobacco garden when the conch shell was blown to alert the village that canoes had been sighted. Each grabbed their war club and ran toward the village. The older women gathered the items they would need and put them in baskets and assigned two children to carry each one. In ten minutes all of them were ready to head toward the center of the forest to await word from their new cacique.

As Bameeta and Gauban each launched their ten smaller canoes, the remaining warriors began rolling eight huge forty-foot-long war canoes toward the water. Bameeta had trained her war chiefs to launch their large canoes and head away from the direction that an enemy was approaching from, and when they were far enough away that they would not be seen, they were to circle around so they could attack from the rear as Bameeta and Gauban used their warriors to keep the enemy occupied.

Bameeta glanced back as she paddled cautiously toward the approaching canoes. Seeing her large canoes swiftly disappearing to the south of Shell Island, as the enemy approached from the north, gave her great confidence.

The enemy canoes had been spotted from the tallest tree near the village, so she knew they had not yet seen her small canoes or the large ones heading to sea. Bameeta and the African sat in their canoes and waited until the enemy canoes appeared as a dark spot on the horizon. She knew that one warrior would be standing on the gunwale and gripping it with his toes as he steadied himself with his paddle. She immediately yelled for her warriors to begin paddling toward the shallow half-mile wide cut that separated Shell Island from Turtleshell Island. They moved a hundred yards ahead and paused when Bameeta yelled for them to stop. She turned and watched; certain that the enemy canoes would follow, but when they passed by and turned toward Shell Island, she laughed. All of her men turned toward her; concern on their faces. She laughed again and smiled, "It is my father, Cacique Ahameke."

A short time later the unmistakable silhouette of her father's dugout was plain for her to see. As usual, Ahameke was standing in the bow, leading the other canoes.

She signaled for the others to return to Shell Island, and when she had her men paddle her canoe next to her father's canoe, Ahameke smiled as he yelled, "you sent them home so you could attack this fleet alone, so you must be a very good warrior and one to fear."

"Yes!" she yelled back, "I am the daughter of the most feared of all Carib." Ahameke smiled and looked at her with pride.

One hour later everyone was drinking cassava beer and laughing about the cacique of all the Carib Indians being attacked by their new cacique. Old G'hana put his leathery arm around Bameeta's shoulder and asked his friend, "were you and your warriors frightened, Ahameke?"

"Not until we spotted the huge war canoes coming at us from the east. We then knew that if we had been an enemy, we would have had a very difficult fight if we were to survive." He turned to his daughter, "Did you devise that bit of strategy?"

"The African and I have talked long into the night how to best be prepared when we are being attacked on this small island."

"So," Ahameke said, "he has learned our language well, has he?"

"Yes," she beamed proudly, as she put her arm around her African's thick muscular neck, "and I his."

"Excellent," Ahameke said and smiled at the African, "he will be able to help plan your attack on the Arawak pig that killed your brother Bapatou before he was even old enough to know the danger he was in."

. . .

Word quickly reached Baracoraima that Carib warriors had raided Arawak villages on the islands of Grenada, St. Lucia, his home island of Trinidad, and even Venezuela, which they believed to also be a huge island. "It was the cannibals." The men carrying the information to their god-like cacique spoke harshly. The young warriors were gesturing in irritation as the older men shook their heads. "They ate some of the young children, because we saw their bones lying near the fire."

One of the young men spoke angrily. "We found all of the other people's bodies laying everywhere. All of them had been mutilated and were bloated with flies on them."

Baracoraima pulled his lips tight, and grit his teeth as his jaw muscles worked. He stared off into the distant haze covering the water. After a few moments he spoke slowly and quietly. "We will teach the Carib cannibals that they will pay when they come to our land." He instructed his sub-chief's to organize a meeting of the caciques from all nearby villages.

One week later, Baracoraima addressed a group of more than two hundred Arawak warriors and chiefs. "Our land has been invaded by the cannibals." He moved his head slowly, and his eyes passed each man, so they would know he was talking to each one personally.

He paused a moment longer as he looked back and forth at the large group of small brown men with slanted eyes that was assembled before him. When he spoke, it was in a very low, deliberately slow, intensely serious tone of voice.

"By this time next year we will have a war fleet such as has never been seen, but we must teach them a lesson now. Then they will stay away until we are ready to attack them and run them from these islands forever."

• • •

Bameeta crossed the channel at night and by dawn had her entire fleet of war canoes concealed in the thick forest and underbrush. With sentries posted during the day, they slept. At night she sent patrols into the interior of Trinidad to locate the Arawak camps where new canoes to replace those burned were under construction. Barely a week later she had already moved her warriors to the southwest tip of the area where Baracoraima's original camp was located. After a long day of sleep and a full night of stealthy observation, she was very satisfied with all of the information they had accumulated. Back in her hiding place before dawn, she spoke quietly to her war chiefs. "We have located the Giant Arawak's camp and will attack tonight. Tell your men of fire to have their coals hot and to keep a close eye on the direction the wind is blowing from, so they will know where to begin. Post new guards every two hours so no warrior tires tonight and dozes off. Remember to thoroughly go over my plan again with your men before dark. They must understand the importance of Camajuya—<u>thunderbolt raid without warning</u>—it will disrupt the burial ceremony that we saw them gathering for tonight. We will kill many and perhaps even the giant, who all say is the man who can not be killed."

. . .

Earlier, while he was visiting a war chief on St Lucia Island, Baracoraima was confronted by a grief such as he had never known. A canoe arrived with word that the woman who had stepped into his mother's place when she was slain by the invading Spaniards, had died.

Edeeshi was once a black slave who had been captured by the Arawak while raiding a Dutch trading vessel. The frail black child was taken and given to Baracoraima's biological parents, who were opposed to the idea of one human owning another as their slave. She was named Edeeshi because she spoke only the African dialect that she learned from her people. The word which she repeated several times while pointing to herself sounded to Ahameke's mother like, Edeeshi.

Baracoraima's mother treated her as another daughter, until the day the old woman was killed by Spaniards. She was pleased that her husband's other wives did the same.

Edeeshi was only twelve years old when taken from the ship, but soon displayed the abilities of an adult. From the first days of her newfound freedom, Edeeshi guarded six-year-old Baracoraima as though he was her very own child. Their relationship grew into a loving mother/son bond. Until the day in Venezuela, when young Baracoraima fled from the Spanish invaders; where you saw him—you saw Edeeshi not far away.

He immediately made preparations to swiftly return to Trinidad, where Edeeshi had lived.

. . .

Many years earlier, when the invading Spaniard's attacked his small village on the northern coast of Venezuela, young Baracoraima reached Trinidad in the company of a group of Arawak warriors. He was sick with worry that Edeeshi had either been killed or was captured by the Spaniards. Although only a child himself he vowed the day that he stepped upon the sandy beach of Trinidad, *I will soon return to our land and kill the men in shiny clothes until I find Edeeshi or am killed myself while trying.* He turned his tear-streaked face to the dark sky above and howled loudly for hours staring at the moon like a crazed wounded animal …iiiiieeeeeeeeeeeeeeeeeeeyaaaaa.

Only days later, when the various groups who had also escaped the slaughter, came together within the cover of the dense growth on Trinidad, Baracoraima heard his name being screamed loudly. Before he even turned toward the source, he knew exactly who it was. "Deeshi, Deeshi"…he screamed the nickname he had given her.

They stood holding one another as Arawak, and Maroon alike watched and smiled. Although they were warriors, a grown male Arawak was very family oriented. It was common to see tears of joy running freely down both black and copper cheeks, at the sight of two loved ones like young Baracoraima and older Edeeshi finding each other after the tragic loss of so many members of their family.

. . .

Now, many years later, Baracoraima remained stoic but was feeling a great personal loss. She had always been a loved member of his village and was grieved by everyone.

Edeeshi's body was adorned in her favorite dress; a bright red silk gown, which was taken from a seized Spanish merchant ship by her adopted son, Baracoraima. On her chest rested a triangular carved stone; a ZEMI—<u>guardian deity of each household</u>—through which the people believed that the Gods transmitted their wishes to them. Her hands were resting upon it as her friends and family passed by in a never-ending circle. Her husband was also a Maroon and had taken only Edeeshi as a wife. He had willingly bred many children among the tribe to increase their numbers, but wanted no other woman as wife. He had been sitting cross-legged at the feet of Edeeshi since the sun rose from the water. He had neither spoke, eaten nor drank, and would not until the sun fell back into the sea and she was placed in her eternal resting place.

Baracoraima himself was digging her deep burial hole. She would be placed in it sitting upright and elaborately adorned with her prized possessions. The village prayer stone would be placed on a post made from a large branch of a gommier tree. It would sit near her grave until the next full moon, when it would be returned to its sacred place within the coconut log hut with palm frond thatched roof. Only the village cacique or the head Arawak Cacique, such as Baracoraima, was allowed to touch their village's Zemi stone—on penalty of death.

When the sun began the long day's journey back to the ocean on the other side of their world, the women had completed a woven honeysuckle vine, chair-like piece, which Edeeshi's body would sit in. Eight Arawak warriors arrived an hour before dusk. Two placed her upon the chair as four others held two poles on their shoulders. The remaining two tied the chair with the vines that had been woven to the seat for that purpose. With Edeeshi sitting lifelike by means of vines tied around her waist and chest, the eight men began a very slow march toward her final resting place. As their journey took them through the village, all fell in behind.

When Baracoraima saw the procession heading toward him, he felt a sadness deep within as never before.

Standing near him was his daughter Atahowee. She loved the old black Maroon as though she had been her paternal grandmother. Unless it had happened when she was too young to remember, Atahowee had never shed a tear, but was now very close. She swallowed the lump in her throat and remained stoic.

When the procession finally arrived at Edeeshi's burial place, Baracoraima stood and silently watched as four designated warriors holding vines attached to her chair lowered her into the ground. He then turned and nodded to another warrior who had accompanied him from his village. The young man approached slowly, carrying an elaborately carved box made from the soft wood of a mahogany tree.

He stopped in front of the mighty Cacique Baracoraima, and was surprised to see tears running freely down his cheeks. *I have learned a very good lesson this day,* he thought as he held the box while Atahowee opened it, *great warriors also cry.*

All watched as the huge cacique removed his ceremonial war-club. All Arawak people had heard about the treasure that Baracoraima had carved while still a young man, but only a few old warriors had ever seen it. All were watching anxiously as he removed the two-foot long club and held it high above his head. Some gasped as the sun reflected off of the huge head at the end. It was carved into the shape of a shark's head and had tigershark teeth imbedded in the mouth. The eyes were emeralds taken from a captured Spanish galleon. Gold coins found on the same galleon had been pounded into thin sheets, which covered the entire shark's head. The exposed wood had been rubbed with the blood of the invaders until it was black and shiny. The hilt was decorated with a thick ring of silver, taken from another invader's vessel, and at the end was attached a huge ingot of gold, which was taken from the pocket of a slaughtered

Catholic priest.

Baracoraima held the beautiful war club high so that all could look upon it. He began talking in a low voice, so all movement and sound immediately stopped. Mothers had trained their children to be completely silent when they made a sign across their lips, and infants had a breast's nipple placed in their mouth.

As he spoke, Baracoraima turned slowly while looking toward the sky. "Oh mighty Baron Samedi, please show Edeeshi the wonders of your underworld as you lead her to the land beyond life on these small islands. We will all miss her very much, but we know that she will enjoy serving you as faithfully as she did her family here." He had come full circle by the time he stopped speaking. He lay prone on the sand and placed the war club on her lap and then placed her right hand on the handle. "All in the afterlife will know you were a great queen here when they see what you bring to the Land-After-Life when you leave the Land-Of-Man."

After rising, he stood a moment looking down at the only mother he had time to really get to know. He then picked up one of the many large gourds, which had been cut in half and lay in a pile nearby. He scooped it full of sand and poured it into the grave. Everyone did the same, and soon a very long procession was slowly circling Edeeshi's grave, with Baracoraima also stooping each time past to fill his gourd. Within an hour the deep hole was filled and had a mound three feet high above.

Not a word was spoken as they all headed toward the campfire, but there was soon conversation and laughter as stories were told about the wonderful black woman they had just sent on her way to the afterlife. Platters filled with tapir, iguana, fish, lobsters, manatee, and crabs, were placed beside platters piled high with cassava bread and sweet potatoes. A huge loggerhead turtle shell was full of every fruit that grew on Trinidad. Huge gourds filled with cassava beer were brought out, and stories about Edeeshi were told far into the night.

Baracoraima's daughter Atahowee turned once again when she heard the noise, but it was too late. During the funeral, Bameeta had watched from the darkness and saw that the giant was at times smiling and talking to the young girl. *She is his daughter or someone that he cares for. It is this young girl that I will kill first.*

Before the girl could scream a warning, Bameeta had clamped her hand on the girl's mouth and cut her throat. One hundred Carib warriors under the command of Raouti and the African rushed in and began bashing heads before the Arawak Indians knew what was happening. When Baracoraima saw that his daughter was being killed, he rushed toward Bameeta, but was hit with a war club by the oldest warrior in Bameeta's fleet. Zeenatuhama knew exactly where to hit a man the size of the giant rushing at his cacique. His hardened war club hit Baracoraima's testicles with a force powerful enough to flatten a normal man for hours, but the old warrior had seen many battles and doubled up when he saw the blow coming. He was still gasping for air when Zeenatuhama's war club was about to come down on his head.

A young Arawak warrior who rushed forward and shoved a long Spanish lance through Zeenatuhama's heart spared Baracoraima's life. He then picked up Baracoraima's fallen Spanish dagger and prepared to defend his cacique or die in the attempt. A signal from Bameeta spared his life.

Bameeta saw that the flames started by her men of fire were already high enough to see them through the thick woods. Her men had done their job and now the wind was helping. The flames would quickly spread across the dry canoes that were completed in preparation for the coming attack on the Caribs, which Baracoraima had planned months earlier. There had been no rain for a long time, and Ahameke used that to launce the raid by his son and daughter.

Bameeta gave the signal and her men turned; as they had been taught when Ahameke explained about the wisdom of Camajuya. *Hit like the lightning bolts do, and then disappear so that you can return another day and strike again.*

Ten men had been left at each of the four Arawak camps they had scouted on the way to Baracoraima's camp. Each group had one man of fire with them. He taught each how to use the smoldering coals they had brought from Shell Island. Their fires were burning the new war canoes and leaping into the night sky when Bameeta's crew paddled along the coast of Trinidad toward their rendezvous place on the coast, a mile north of the last village. Her warriors were there now, burning more of Baracoraima's new war canoes.

Before midnight all of Raouti and Bameeta's warriors, except for old Zeenatuhama, were in their long canoes and heading toward their home camps on Shell Island and Martinique.

It was a raid that would be repeated in legend, about the only female Carib Cacique ever, and the part she played in defeating the legendary Arawak Cacique Baracoraima. She would become one of the great legends among her people, and stories about her daring raids would be told long after she died as a very old woman.

~ Guerrilla Warfare ~

The guerrilla warfare plan that Baracoraima laid out for his very best band of warriors to accomplish would have extremely disastrous consequences for the Carib Indians who would eventually live on Dominica, Martinique, and St. Vincent, for centuries. At this time, however, the bulk of the Carib Indians only inhabited Martinique and several smaller islands nearby. The impact of the terrifying raid on the Carib Indians would initially be confined to those on Martinique, but would eventually spread to other islands. The results of the Arawak Indians' action would one day backfire and cause them to wonder about the wisdom of Baracoraima's decision.

Two hundred Arawak warriors sat silently listening as the old cacique explained his plan. When he finished, he spoke again in the deadly tone that even frightened some of his own younger warriors. "Now go to your women, and tell them to begin weaving the baskets, so that you can soon go to the big island of Venezuela and begin the hunt."

One month later, Baracoraima stood on the beach and watched, as two of his new forty-foot-long dugout canoes headed toward the east to pay the Carib stronghold on Martinique a visit.

Each canoe was commanded by a war cacique that Baracoraima personally chose for his stealth and wisdom. Each canoe had twenty of the best paddlers among the entire Arawak population that was living on Trinidad. These paddlers were also warriors, and each was very much respected for their strength and durability. Once the canoes were loaded with their deadly cargo, they were moved to the beach on roller logs. The logs behind the canoe were then continuously moved forward and placed beneath the bow by some, as other members of the tribe pushed the canoes. They rolled smoothly from the site in the jungle where they had been constructed, to the edge of the water. Before rolling the canoes forward into the water, Baracoraima spoke to the two groups. "Move swiftly through the night, but conceal yourselves on a small island with dense jungle before the sun arrives. You must not be discovered before delivering our gift to the Carib cannibals. When you have completed your mission, move swiftly toward home, because we will need many warriors when our new fleet of war canoes, to replace those burned again by the cannibals, is ready. Go swiftly now, and we will sacrifice ten fat parrots to Guabancex every day that you are gone, so that she will bless your voyage."

For three nights the men paddled through calm night seas, and rested during each day. They finally arrived at a small, uninhabited island lying only a few miles from Martinique. They concealed the two canoes before sunrise, and again rested during the day. As darkness descended across the area, the Arawak warriors silently moved from the jungle into the sea, and once again headed toward their destination. Within the hour they arrived unseen and unheard on the south tip of Martinique.

The second canoe continued with their deadly cargo toward a spot several miles farther north. The chief and ten warriors guarded the canoe, as the other ten carried the baskets into the jungle, and carefully lay them down. They cautiously opened the lids and swiftly departed.

The vine baskets were unique to the Arawak, so the Caribs would know who had brought them the gifts. Both canoes then paddled furiously toward St. Lucia, where there were several large Arawak villages. They rested in the dense jungle until noon the next day, and then headed south toward home. They made one stop on a small island in the Grenadines to catch fish, crabs, and lobsters to fill empty stomachs and rest, and then immediately pushed on toward Trinidad.

The two canoes full of Arawak warriors went offshore, and bypassed Grenada, where they could have enjoyed a well deserved rest. So anxious were all aboard to get home, that they paddled directly toward Trinidad.

Baracoraima and the other caciques met them, and all were very pleased to hear that the men had not been seen, and had delivered their gifts without incident.

A great feast was called for, so the women immediately began making preparations. After enough food for all was placed on wooden benches, the women began rubbing scented flowers on their naked bodies. They continued this as the warriors ate, knowing that the men would soon smell their loveliness and begin chasing them into the jungle.

Two nights later, all listened as the men sat around a tribal fire and told their stories. "We carried the baskets into the jungle near their villages, and opened them so the hundreds of deadly fer-de-lance vipers that we caught on the big island of Venezuela could escape. Many of the cannibals will die horribly, and we will have fewer enemies."

It was but one of the many guerrilla warfare strategies that Baracoraima conceived, which helped to create a legend that will forever be told about the cunning mind of the huge Arawak chief.

Baracoraima and his people worked tirelessly on the new fleet of large war canoes during the entire year following the delivery of the snakes. Even though his dream of building a vast fleet of canoes with which to destroy the Caribs was twice destroyed, he still unwaveringly held to his dream of forever ridding the Caribbean of the dreaded cannibals.

. . .

Less than one week after the snakes had been deposited on Martinique, the first victim stumbled into her small village.

A twelve-year-old Carib girl came running, and was holding her arm. She found her mother, and told about her encounter with the goddess of rainbows and her husband, both of which materialized as snakes. "I was picking the small sour limes that you want for our fish dinner, when AIDA WEDO—kissed my arm." She held her arm up so her mother could see. The entire arm was already swollen, and the mother instructed her son to find the medicine man. "DAMBALLA—husband of Aida Wedo—was with her, and kissed me too." She lifted her foot and pointed at her big toe, which was the size of a small cucumber. "We sacrificed a pig and many chickens before my marriage to Ahazumi, so I know that Aida Wedo would not harm me, but my entire body hurts very bad, mama."

Before the girl's thirty-five-year-old husband and the medicine man arrived, she was in a coma. Her inflamed body had already begun convulsing, and a very short time later she died. It was the beginning of a nightmare for the Carib Indians who had lived on Martinique for many years. During the first full year that the tribe of Arawak Indians under Baracoraima's command was concentrating on rebuilding their war fleet, more than one hundred Caribs living on Martinique died from fer de lance viper venom. As catastrophic as the encounter with the deadly vipers was, it was nothing compared to what was just beyond the horizon.

The large white sails that soon appeared in the distance were bringing a new and terrifying nightmare. It was one that would alter the course of the Carib's future, and also that of the Arawak natives.

• • •

Sir Thomas Warner's fleet of English ships moved boldly into the vast and poorly charted Caribbean Sea with only limited information concerning the islands and the natives who occupied them. The sparse information that was available had been gathered from sailing tradesmen of various nations who were continuously searching the wet world for new sources of trade goods. After gathering information from French, Dutch, Portuguese and Spanish traders, who regularly passed through these islands en route to more lucrative markets in the east, the information attained was often so inaccurate that it was essentially useless.

Sir Thomas Warner lowered the long looking glass after intensely scrutinizing the island of Saint Christopher. It was named by the explorer, Christopher Columbus, who under the flag of Castile had again been exploring the Caribbean islands in the year 1493. "This must be the island that the disgusting scoundrel, Columbus, discovered."

A week after anchoring his fleet in the largest of the many lagoons, Sir Warner's navigator cautiously informed him that researching his many logbooks indicated that the island was indeed the same one that the famous explorer named after his patron, Saint Christopher. A moment later the navigator turned and headed back toward his cabin, but stopped when he heard Sir Warner call his name.

"Yessir."

"From this moment on," the short, rotund, aging English gentleman commanded, "this island shall be known as Saint Kitts."

Almost four hundred years later—it remains St. Kitts.

A week later, Sir Thomas Warner gave the fleet orders to haul their anchors and follow him. Atop 3,793 ft. Mount Liamuiga, an Arawak lookout spotted the giant canoes with white wings leaving their harbor and ran swiftly to tell his cacique the good news. The old Arawak Indian had seen the arrival of the white men to his home in Venezuela when he was a young boy. Before he was fifteen they had returned many times, and each visit left his peaceful village in ruins. Most of the old people were slaughtered, and many young men and women had been taken away in chains. Children who were old enough to soon be useful as slaves were spared—infants were killed.

The old Arawak silently followed the young warrior to the point that the sea could be easily seen. After watching the English sails on the horizon getting steadily smaller, he turned to limp painfully back to the village. After several steps he turned to the young warrior, "it is not the last that we have seen of those white men."

. . .

From atop St. Lucia's 3,619 ft. Mount Piton, an Arawak lookout spotted a white dot far in the distance and alerted his fellow lookouts by blowing into the chipped-off end of a conch shell. Each heard the signal, and as one of their friends continued watching their assigned sections of the vast Caribbean Sea surrounding the Arawak stronghold, they hastened to find out what had been seen. They arrived to find the guards on the east side of the mountain intently watching the white dot. "It has grown much larger since I signaled you." The three east side lookouts, and several others who had quickly arrived from the other three sides of the mountaintop, watched in awe. "It is Guantuava," one warrior said, "and she has been sent by Guabancex to warn her favorite people that a storm is coming."

All silently nodded their heads in agreement.

"I think it is Ghede," another speculated, "and she has come to destroy all of us for putting those deadly snakes on the island where the fierce Carib Cacique Ahameke lives." Group fear caused them to again nod in confirmation.

"No," another said, "it is Marinette and her husband Ti-Jean Petro. She is the helper to the earth goddess Nana Buruku, and she is mad because we Arawak have cut down so many gommier trees to make war canoes. She has finally come to send us all to live with Ghede."

"Look!" The man who had blown the signal conch was pointing far to the north of the white spot, and then moved his arm to the south. "It is none of them, because there are too many." All of the warriors moved their eyes back and forth as the white dot not only continued to get larger, but also grew in number. When finally the south guard spoke, all listened as their eyes grew wide.

"It is the white men in shiny clothes. I have heard stories that they come upon great winged birds from the land beyond the sun." As they fearfully watched the horizon, the white dots continued multiplying. "Some have said that they come up out of the ocean in canoes larger than our village, and have many warriors with sticks that can kill us when we do not yet see them."

By the time he finished telling about the strange white men; Sir Thomas Warner's fleet appeared to the natives as though it was one long white spot on the horizon. Before the sun had positioned itself directly above St Lucia, the group of English ships had found their way through the reef, and was entering the harbor.

The harbor was protected by the twin peaks of Mount Gros Piton and the smaller Mount Petit Piton, rising 200 feet less in height, but no less beautiful to seamen searching for protection from a wild and angry Caribbean Sea. They rose precipitously from cobalt blue water and appeared to be a formidable refuge; should the need arise. They had stood as they were since being formed after a volcanic eruption 30 million years earlier.

"Captain Hargrave," Sir Warner yelled in his thundering ostentatious voice, "have my signalman contact the warships so that I might give them an order." Sir Warner never took his eyes from the island, and completely ignored his captain who remained standing at rigid attention saluting his employer. When Sir Warner finally noticed the man, he waved his short flabby arm impatiently, and screamed, "Get on with the order I just gave you, and do not stand there like a bloody fool, you dolt."

The timid captain, commissioned as a favor by a friend of his wealthy father, dropped his tired salute and rushed off in a nervous spastic flailing of thin arms and legs, screaming repeatedly and loudly in his small tinny voice, "***signalman, signalman.***"

Captain Hargrave soon returned to the rear cabin to which his employer had retired for a glass of sherry. He stood silently, eyes twitching as his head jerked spastically to the left, ending each time with the small black beard on his weak, incestuous chin pointed upwards, toward some unknown object on the beautifully hand carved mahogany wall panels, as his gaping mouth almost touched his left shoulder.

Once the cut crystal glass in Sir Warner's gloved hand was full, and the diminutive old Chinaman had returned to ironing his master's clothes, the captain spoke. "My lord, the signalman has contacted the commander of your fleet of warships, and he awaits your orders."

"Very well, send them this message. As we lower our canvas, the warships are to pass us by, then line up and fire one complete broadside from every vessel at the same time, directly into this island's interior. I want each and every cannibal savage living on this island to know that my ships have arrived to take possession."

When the English cannons erupted, and their huge steel balls pummeled the interior of St Lucia, three thousand Arawak Indians had already followed their old cacique's instructions and fled swiftly to the top of Mount Petit Piton, and another two thousand to Mount Gros Piton. Only a small amount of actual damage to the villages of these natives occurred, but as the steel balls rained down, a fierce hatred began burning deep within the hearts of the Arawak Indians watching from the mountaintops.

A few wise old caciques had survived similar incidents along the coast of mainland South America, before fleeing the invading Spanish conquerors. As soon as the English ships were sighted, they sent young warriors running to all of the small villages, instructing the people to go to the mountaintops. "Tell them to carry food and water so that we will be able to survive until these invaders leave and we can return to our villages."

The young warriors ran swiftly from one village to the next, warning all who would listen. Most villagers ran but there were a few old people who walked slowly and wailed in grief, while praying to a variety of gods and goddesses as they climbed higher and higher. A few of the others who stubbornly remained in their village were either crippled or killed in the shower of iron balls.

. . .

A large tribe of Arawak Indians had successfully invaded the island many years earlier, and easily conquered the few Carib Indians who had been living on St Lucia since being run from their homes along the coast of South America. Those who did not flee were killed, and the Carib Indians moved north to Martinique where there were huge Carib villages. This event fueled a burning hatred that already existed between these two tribes.

The invading Europeans had not yet encountered the Carib Indians. The many horror stories they heard of cannibals inhabiting every island throughout the Caribbean Sea were carried mostly on the lips of traveling merchants. The many guerrilla warfare tactics of hit and run, plus leaving behind the unmistakable signs of cannibalism, adopted by the Carib Indians, was having the desired effect. All European ships now entered the Caribbean islands with extreme caution, as fear gnawed at their minds. Even the Arawak Indians, who had been fighting the Carib Indians from the first days they each entered the Caribbean, were now trying to get every village to post a guard in the tallest tree to alert the village when a Carib canoe was sighted.

The arriving European vessels had been in contact with seafaring Spaniards who told of Christopher Columbus' ghastly encounters with the local natives. These tales of horror were from the distant past, so were shrugged off as attempts by the Spanish Crown to discourage attempts by other nations to explore the Caribbean.

The British were now about to learn that the stories of ferocious Caribbean warriors were not exaggerated. The French, who moved into the area soon after the English departed, would also have a vast collection of stories to tell. They too would encounter the small bronze warriors with slanted eyes who fought without fear, and always left vivid evidence of their cannibalism for the enemy to digest.

When the Arawak lookouts brought the alarming news to their island cacique, he instructed his warriors to begin a plan, which he had devised much earlier in the event that white men appeared near his island base on St Lucia. He and his people would soon learn that there were many white men other than those in shiny clothes that they would be forced to deal with. Cacique Zeteena looked directly into the dark eyes of his second in command. "Ahokana, assemble three of your men and tow all canoes to the rear of our island and put them in the jungle. After concealing them, return in one canoe and carry it to the top of Mount Gros Piton, where most of our people will by now be assembled.

Women who had brought small children were herded into several small caves where they could keep them from being heard. The warriors constantly circulated among the others and reminded them that the white men on the boats in the harbor must not see them. For two weeks they ate dried fish, roots, fruits, and anything else that did not require a fire. Only men designated by Cacique Zeteena were allowed to move about during the day. Those few did so stealthily, and therefore were never seen by the English invaders.

Sir Thomas Warner had his young cabin boy locate Captain Hargrave and inform him that he should come immediately to his private quarters. The meek, incompetent little man soon arrived and was standing at rigid attention; head twitching spastically as his employer issues new orders. "It has become obvious to me lieutenant, tha...

Captain Hargrave interrupted nervously in a barely audible voice, "captain, sir."

Sir Warner spun about and stared at the man. "What?"

The captain's voice cracked like a misbehaved child's; caught in some mischievous deed. "I'm a captain, sir."

Sir Warner stood five feet-six inches in his stocking feet. He glared up at the skinny, now almost petrified young man. "When I'm on this boat you will always be Lieutenant Hargrave. I spent a fortune to have this fleet constructed in an effort to make my name known from one end of the extended British Kingdom to the other. You will continue to refer to me as Sir Warner, but make no mistake; I am the captain of this vessel and admiral to all of the ships in this fleet." He leaned forward to emphasize his point. "Is that understood, **lieutenant**?" While slamming his small pudgy hand down on the top of his heavy, elaborately carved desk, barely causing items to move, he loudly emphasized the last word.

"Yessir!" The quavering officer saluted, and continued to

hold it to his cap long after Sir Warner turned away. "It has become obvious to me, lieutenant," he continued in an irritated voice, "that the natives who once lived on this island have fled." He turned to see the man still holding the salute to the bill of his odd, rumpled little cap. "Good Lord man, stop holding that bloody salute. Did they teach you to do that at the Naval Academy?"

"I didn't go to the Naval Academy, sir."

"Certainly doesn't surprise me." After ringing the small brass bell to summon his Chinese servant to come and pour him another glass of imported Portuguese sherry, he raised the cut crystal to his thick lips and closed his swollen eyes as he emptied it. "Ahhhhhh yes! Wonderful sherry they make in Lisbon." After commanding the Chainman to refill the crystal glass, he continued. "We have wasted too much time searching for those damn cannibals, if they even exist. Send a message to each vessel that there will be only one nighttime guard required on deck. I want every common seaman to immediately begin getting each ship in top condition for my entrance into Venezuela. They must rest at night so they can begin at dawn after breakfast and not stop until it is time for their evening meal." He emptied the glass again before adding, "I want this flotilla to shine like no English fleet of ships ever has." He watched as the servant removed the glass stopper from the decanter to refill his master's glass, and then spoke menacingly once again. "Is that understood?" When the beanpole captain began to raise his arm to salute, Sir Thomas Warner literally screamed at him, "**stop that silly saluting**." He paused then added, "unless of course, we're among the crew." He waved his small pudgy hand with manicured fingernails as though he was dismissing a servant. "Get on with it man, get on with it."

Ahokana sat beside Zeteena in the dark moonless night. Zeteena's voice was so low that Ahokana leaned toward his cacique. "Have men been observing the white men on the big canoes?"

"Yes! Each night for a full hand, many have paddled

silently in the night near their giant canoes and watched. There is now only one white man on watch above as the others sleep below. Last night several canoes went with two people, so one could see if he could climb up the tall sides of the large canoes, while the other moved away into the darkness."

"And our warriors succeeded?"

"Yes, easily, and they could have climbed into each of the enemy's large canoes and silently killed the guard, but they returned to their dugout unseen as you instructed."

"Very good. Have the women been busy?"

"Yes! All is ready."

"Excellent! Then we will teach these white men a lesson that those who survive can carry with them to tell as they sit around their campfires. Tomorrow night while the moon is resting in the sea will be the perfect time to strike."

"Our warriors have been tending the fires near the hidden canoes on the other side of the island. They will bring the glowing coals and tree sap in all of our small canoes tomorrow night. I must go to the women now and tell them to prepare the baskets."

While Ahokana and Zeteena were busy preparing for the following night's surprise visit to the English ships, Sir Warner was finishing a lengthy entry in his log.

'In summation, I believe we have been taken in by the imaginations of seamen from countries less courageous than our stout English sailors. We have searched high and low for signs of the dreaded cannibals; reputed to inhabit these islands along the route to Venezuela and other points of that continent. My continuing search of the islands along the route to Maracaibo will once and for all time, put an end to the rumors that spread from the lips of a frightened foreign sailor to the ears of the next sailor he meets. There are no signs of ferocious cannibals to prevent England from creating settlements throughout this area. The few natives that lived on this island must have fled in terror in their small canoes at the first sight of our majestic fleet. If His Majesty will authorize a fleet of English immigrants, all of these islands will soon become the property of The British Crown. Before leaving this area, my plans are to conduct a ceremony on the large island nearby and name it Warner Island. The ship's carpenter is crafting a sign for the first town, which will be named Thomasville'.

He put his quill and ink away, snuffed out the lamp, and slept like a newborn.

Zeteena held the war club next to his leg as the canoe approached the huge English vessel. War canoes silently carried his Arawak warriors toward nineteen other English ships. He had chosen those ships nearest the ship commanded by the short fat man. From the top of the mountain, he had been watching him through a telescope. The long looking glass was Zeteena's most prized possession. He had taken it from a Spanish merchant ship that he and his warriors had attacked, looted, and burned, two years previously. Zeteena correctly selected Sir Warner as the leader of the group of ships that had entered the protected harbor of his island. It would eventually be named St Lucia, but during the time that Sir Thomas Warner brought his fleet of English ships into the harbor, it was known by all as Zeteena Island. Even other Arawak Indians were cautious when approaching it.

A seasoned warrior commanded each Arawak war canoe. They had all listened intently as Zeteena explained his strategy to defeat the huge fleet that had invaded his stronghold. Zeteena was half a century old and had battled foreign invaders many times. Within his bronze chest beat a heart filled with revenge. As a child he had watched from concealment among the bushes near his village in the Venezuelan jungle, as a large group of invading Spaniards slaughtered his entire family. From that day forth, all white men were his enemy. When he was certain that all of his orders were understood, each warrior assembled his crew and passed the plan to them.

Twenty war canoes now carried two-hundred Arawak warriors that were armed with clubs lined with tiger shark and mako shark teeth, an assortment of Spanish swords and daggers, plus a burning hatred of all invading people—and also two weapons of inestimable terror.

The twenty canoes gathered a quarter of a mile from the large ship commanded by Sir Warner. At a barely audible bird-trilling signal from Zeteena, they headed toward their assigned target. A warrior in each of the war canoes began rhythmically dropping a small river stone overboard. Each canoe arrived near a designated ship and remained in the dark as the warrior continued dropping a stone into the sea. When the last of the one hundred stones in each time-counter's gourd was dropped, every canoe that was silently sitting alongside an English ship became lighter as the warriors climbed. One warrior in each canoe carried a sand-filled turtle shell with glowing coals and a protected bundle of dry tinder enclosed in tree sap—semi-hard and ready to burst into sticky flames. Two others, each carried a basket filled with twenty deadly, venomous, very agitated, fer-de-lance vipers, many of which were longer than the tallest man among them. The tactic that had worked so well against their enemy the Carib, was about to be repeated.

The Arawak were honing guerrilla warfare skills that would still be used by modern warriors, many centuries later. Terrorize the enemy and then swiftly kill him in the confusion.

The most critical task would be given to the two best climbers in each canoe. All would rest on the skill of one warrior in each canoe. Success would rely on their ability to climb the sides of the English ships and silently kill the single sentry. The other climbed aboard and stealthily searched for the entrances used by the English seamen to go below. As soon as the guard was dead, a signal was given for all but one warrior to board the ship on vine ropes dropped by the first two warriors. One must remain to tend the canoe.

After the lone sentry was killed, and the crew quarters located, the third warrior to step onto the ship's deck was the fire-bearer. He removed the honeysuckle vine rope from his waist and lowered it to the young canoe tender. After it was tied, he hauled his turtle shell and kindling aboard. As the other warriors scrambled up the side, he already had the kindling in place and the hot coals among it. By blowing on them, he soon had flames racing through the dry wood. The wooden English ships had enjoyed a lengthy period of dry weather and were ready to greedily accept the flames.

All movement by the Arawak had been done silently; unheard by the exhausted English seamen sleeping below. The Captain's quarters at the rear of the ship were also located.

As the flames raced up the freshly painted sides of the Captain's quarters on each vessel, the hatch to the crew's quarters was opened and a basket of deadly vipers was dropped down the steps; followed moments later by a basket of sticky flaming resin. The largest warrior in each group put his shoulder to the task of smashing in the door to the Captain's area, so another smaller basket of snakes could be tossed in. As the sleep-subdued man stumbled about in search of his weapon, he was struck numerous times by several of the fer-de-lance—most longer than he was tall.

Barely minutes after the twenty canoes came alongside the English ships flames were spreading across the rear quarters of all twenty vessels. Men ran screaming from their sleeping area onto the deck. Many still had vipers attached to their arms and face as war clubs crushed the heads of those who had escaped the snakes.

The bronze warriors carefully avoided the venomous snakes as they swiftly and unceremoniously dispatched each Englishman who frantically scrambled from below. When the leader of the group was satisfied that the fire was burning out of control, he signaled his Arawak men and they evacuated the ship.

The youngest warrior had been left in the canoe, and he

now paddled it from where he sat waiting nearby in case his friends were forced to jump from the invader's large canoe.

After the twenty Arawak canoes were beached on the island, it was learned that not one warrior was lost or wounded. It was a great victory over the invading enemy, and was made even better when daylight found the rest of the ships hastily raising their sails to depart.

One aspect of the raid on the English ships that helped the Arawak in one way but hurt in another was that Sir Warner's log was not read until years later when it was found on the burned wreck in a sealed container. Every nation who had ever heard the tales of cannibals and other ferocious natives told by passing sailors of many nations still believed every word. Well-armed escorts would regularly accompany the merchant ships from the various nations. All evidence of the tactics used by the Arawak Indians was burned, so the Europeans would not learn of their use of the deadly fer-de-lance for a very long time.

. . .

Atupi was a wise teacher who stopped often so that his young students could absorb the information, and also ask questions. His only demand at such times was that they stand one at a time and wait until he told them to speak.

"Yes, Podomani." From the moment that he took the five boys to the mountaintop, he considered the powerfully built young man one of the best he had ever taught.

"Ahameke needed many more warriors, so when his son Raouti carried the African men and women back with him I believe it helped his village very much."

Atupi looked first at the boy, and then at each of the other four. "Yes, Raouti could have continued raiding Arawak villages, and put many more women in their canoes. He was young, but already a wise leader. He decided that the most important course of action was to save the Africans so they would become members of his village. Raouti also knew that he must immediately carry the information that he had learned back to Ahameke as swiftly as he and his men could paddle." He said no more and remained silent as the boys thought about his answer. Podomani sat down when Ahanabi stood. "Yes, Ahanabi?"

"Did Yemaya ride with Raouti through the bad storms to get him home to The People safely?"

Atupi walked to the boy and placed his leather-like hand on his shoulder. "The gods always come to The People whenever they need help, because we alone are their children." The boy looked up at the old warrior and smiled as he shook his small head up and down. He sat back down with the smile still on his face.

"Now I will tell you what happens to people like the Arawak who have no true gods to help and protect them."

. . .

After the remaining Africans were rescued, Ahameke called his war chiefs to sit at his fire and drink cassava beer. When his wives had served each of his guests a large gourd filled with the pungent, earthen-cooled beverage, Ahameke spoke. "We must soon use the information that Raouti and Bameeta returned with. We must go with many warriors to Trinidad and destroy the rest of the big war canoes that the Arawak are building."

"Yes!" Said one of his wives' brothers, who was his most trusted war chief. "We must not allow them to create a fleet of the large canoes, like those that Raouti and Bameeta burned."

Another chief spoke. "Baracoraima is a very powerful cacique, and with a fleet such as we now know that he is attempting to construct, he will be a very difficult warrior to defeat." He smiled slyly, "if he is allowed to succeed."

"Some say that he cannot be killed because he is a god." One of Ahameke's new Maroon war chiefs was known to always say what was on his mind, even though he still had difficulty expressing himself in his new language. The big African had distinguished himself by his fierce fighting tactics in two small skirmished with the Arawak Indians, which they had stumbled upon while reconnoitering St.

Lucia, prior to their invasion of the small island. "I tell you this now, Cacique Ahameke, if I meet him in battle either he or I will die."

Ahameke scowled momentarily but a wide smile soon replaced it. "The legend that he can not be killed is one that we will send home to Ghede." He paused and narrowed his slanted eyes, "in the dead body of Baracoraima."

"Yes my cacique," one of the other warriors said, "when the giant Arawak sleeps forever at the bottom of the ocean, we will all live better lives."

"Drink beer tonight then rest well, because tomorrow we leave for Trinidad."

. . .

The Caribs were never able to pronounce his African name, so Ahameke decided to rename the huge African. Late one evening while visiting his daughter on Shell Island, several months after Bameeta and the African arrived there, Bameeta walked hand-in-hand with the huge black to the fire, where Ahameke was sitting with his old friend, G'hana. "Father, you will soon have a fierce grandson to sit on your knee and listen as you tell him about the battles that you have had with your many enemies." Ahameke had seen his daughter and the African sneaking into the jungle while still on Martinique, and approved immensely of her choice. He looked first at her and then the African, and smiled. "If he fights like his father, the boy's birth will become a day of mourning for the Arawak."

"The other African warriors say that he was a fighter with great skill and courage the first time he entered battle as a young boy." She turned and looked up at her African. "He carried home a head of the enemy after the first battle."

Ahameke stood and waited until the stiffness left his legs, then stepped forward and placed his hand on the black's shoulder, and spoke directly to him. "My daughter has waited for the right warrior, and I believe she has now found him. You have only one fault, and I am going to fix that right now." The African was rapidly learning the Carib language, and Ahameke could see the look of confusion in the man's eyes, so he continued without waiting to see if he understood what he had just said. "We have all tried to speak your African name, but it sounds like the noises the guinea hens make. From this moment on you are Guaban, because you are a great storm on both land and water."

After listening intently, the African grinned wide and repeated his name. "Gawban."

"Yes!" Ahameke smiled at the man, "I hope you have many sons, and if you have a daughter I hope she is fierce like her mother."

Ahameke turned when his friend G'hana's oldest wife said something that made the other wives giggle.

G'hana scowled, "what are you mumbling about, old cassava butcher?"

The wrinkled old woman pointed and giggled even harder. "With something the size of that hanging between his legs, there will be too many children for this small island."

Bameeta was not surprised when Ahameke told her that they would soon be leaving for Trinidad. "After receiving that information brought by you and Raouti, I have decided that we must swiftly attack the Arawak before they can recover." Ahameke was known as a war cacique that did not spend time worrying about a problem. His response was always swift and brutal. "We are going to carry the Arawak some gifts from G'hede."

When the moon had once again become a full round ball, it shined down on thirty Carib war canoes being prepared to carry fifteen warriors in each, with the huge black African, Guaban, in command of one and Bameeta another. Many of the rescued African warriors had learned how to swim, and were ready and very willing to assume a position as warrior in a canoe. Ahameke would, as always, be in the front of the lead canoe. He began a tradition many years earlier that remained long after his death. Any chief, who could take the lead away from the commanding cacique's canoe, would at that moment become the new cacique, and the ex-cacique was expected to be his most loyal follower.

. . .

Atupi paused before continuing, because every group of young Carib boys always had questions at this point in the story about their people's history. He turned to listen as Podomani spoke.

"Why did the crazy white men want to kill all of The People?"

"We did not know then that they are like the ants when food is left uncared for. They came in such numbers to take the land from The People, so they would have enough room for their own kind. To accomplish that, they must first kill all who are living where they decide to settle and built their village."

When Bomatana spoke next, Atupi wondered what fears the young boy would have seen in the story. *He fears all of the spirits and gods, but will eventually learn that the white men are the ones to fear, because they are more terrible than all of the bad spirits and evil gods.*

"Was it not Baron Samedi who sent the white men in shiny clothes to cast The People into the underworld?"

"We do not know where they came from, or who sent them to kill The People." Atop the mountain, Atupi paused to look out across the beautiful blue water, which was being washed clean of the night blackness by a bright morning sun. He always marveled at how easily his dark world could be brightened and made lovely by—Nana Buruku—<u>Earth Goddess</u>.

Atupi looked at his young group and grinned. "What we do know is that Ahameke, his son Raouti, and his daughter Bameeta often made them wish that they had remained in the part of the world where they came from."

The young group of students enjoyed learning about how their people dealt with the invading white men, but all of the young Caribs were anxious to hear the story of the great battle between their Cacique Ahameke, and the giant Arawak, Cacique Baracoraima. Training by their mothers had prepared them well for their time with the old teacher. They each understood that becoming a great Carib warrior required many traits. "You must learn to be very patient," their mothers had told them many times, "you must listen carefully to Atupi, and not ask too many questions. Your mouth will teach you nothing, but you will learn all with your ears if you keep them open."

. . .

Ahameke circulated among his men and watched as they each completed the task that he had given them a week earlier. "I believe we will have enough today to begin preparing our ambush. We will make the Arawak wish they had allowed the men in shiny clothes to make slaves of them."

Three days later, Ahameke led his fleet of thirty war canoes south toward St Lucia, where he knew that the Arawak moved freely between the small islands as they traded amongst themselves.

A paddle beating lightly against the side of his canoe in the darkness brought the sub-chiefs paddling to Ahameke's dugout. "We will conceal our warriors in the dense growth of St Vincent and lay in wait until the Arawak pass by, on their way to Grenada." Ahameke spoke quietly to his chiefs as they all gathered around his unique seventy-foot long dugout, in their smaller fifty-foot canoes. "Tell your men to be certain that all is ready when the enemy is spotted."

Two sentries were instructed to climb a palm tree at each end of their encampment, and cut out enough fronds so that they and their relief would be able to sit hidden inside and watch the horizon. Four days from the moment the sky lightened, until it was too dark to see, two pairs of eyes scanned the sea constantly.

An hour after dawn on the fifth day, the sentry on the south end sent a trilling whistle to his chief who sat nearby, leaning against a coconut palm. The old sub-chief looked up and waited until his warrior signaled with his hands that there was a group of Arawak canoes about to move past the island they were on.

Moments later, the old sub-chief was standing before his cacique. Ahameke listened to him then turned to his war chief and issued an order before following the old chief to the base of the palm that his sentry was in. He looked up at the sentry who was intently watching something on the sea. A moment later he looked down toward Ahameke, and using hand signs, let him know that it was definitely Arawak canoes that he was watching. Within one minute, fifteen of the thirty war canoes, that were now cleared of dead palm fronds, which had been used to camouflage them. Each had seven warriors standing on both sides, and the chief waiting at the rear. The second sentry was summoned, and he took his position beside Ahameke, who was ready to lift the stern of the dugout and rush through the forest to the sandy beach.

The old sub-chief, and the sentry who had spotted the Arawak dugouts, joined the war party moments later. The old chief stood silent beside the canoe a moment before talking. "The enemy will soon pass by us very close, my cacique."

Ahameke turned to the old war chief and spoke quietly, "have the reserve warriors prepare their canoes as soon as we are in the water, but do not come out unless you see that there are other Arawak canoes coming to join their people." Ahameke waited until the enemy had passed beyond where his warriors were concealed. He felt certain that a group of Arawak traders would not be watching behind as often as they should while paddling and he could be upon them before they even realized the danger they were in.

He was correct, and moments after rushing with their large war canoes across the beach and into the water, his much better trained paddlers were soon closing the gap. When Ahameke's lead dugout canoe was spotted by the Arawak, the men he pursued tried in vain to open the distance between them and their enemy. Shouts from the chiefs, "cannibals are behind us. Paddle faster, faster," created only more terror among his young men and caused them to paddle less effectively.

The scouts had scrambled back up the trees, and yelled to the old war chief that they saw no other canoes.

When Ahameke's men brought his dugout to within two feet beside the first Arawak vessel, the Arawak men lay their paddles down and picked up their wooden war clubs. With the Carib war canoes beside them, the Arawaks were certain that they were now going to fight for their lives, and were surprised to see two Carib warriors in each, stand up and prepare to throw a large basket into each of the Arawak canoes.

The specially woven, basket-like vine container landed exactly as they had during the many practice throws in the Carib training camp from which they had come. The special design that Ahameke himself had created, worked perfectly, and the moment it rested against the bottom of the dugout, the basket fell open and dozens of extremely irritated fer-de-lance vipers immediately began striking every nearby Arawak.

All knew that there was little hope of surviving a strike by the most poisonous snake in the Caribbean. Since they were captured and used as a terror tactic against the Carib by the Arawak, they had multiplied quite rapidly on the Caribbean islands where Arawak warriors had dumped them earlier. With a gestation period of only four months, and a yield of up to eighty young vipers, there were now thousands of them on several islands. The snakes could swim quite well, and also often hid among trade goods carried to other places. Many grew rapidly to almost eight feet in length, and were the source of many nightmares; a nightmare that always ended in an extremely painful death.

Each group of Ahameke's warriors had discharged their deadly cargo and pulled away to sit in their canoes and watch the Arawak Indians as they leaped into the water, many with a viper still attached, with its fangs deeply embedded in their flesh. Many were able to leap into the water before being struck by the snakes—only to be killed by a Carib war club. When a very young boy was about to have his head bashed in, Ahameke yelled. "**Do not kill the boy.** Bring him into your canoe and tie his hands to his feet behind his back." He pointed to another boy flailing the calm water with his arms. "Save that one also."

When the two youths had been securely tied, Ahameke and his men sat back and sipped coconut water as his other warriors paddled from one Arawak to the next. Some were swimming in hopes of escaping their inevitable fate at the hands of the Carib, while others who had been bitten by the vipers simply tread water in a helpless slow-motion death dance. One swift swing of an ironwood war club and the dance was ended.

"Use your paddle to keep the vipers from entering our canoes." Ahameke stood and yelled his instructions to the band of youthful warriors. This was the first taste of battle for many and he realized that they were eager but also inexperienced. "Push the vipers toward the island because they can swim very well, and perhaps we will return one day soon and gather their children for another surprise delivery to the Arawak."

There were soon very few Arawak alive in the water. Some of the Caribs continued killing the few who were still alive, while the others turned the Arawak canoes over to dump out the remaining snakes, and push them toward the islands. They then up-righted the dugouts and cautiously began bailing them dry. Very carefully they gathered the floating bales of goods that their enemy had been carrying and placed them in the prize canoes.

The surrounding water was turning red as desperately struggling Indians were slaughtered. Large grey shadows were seen moving beneath the terrified Arawaks, and as if a primordial dinner bell had rung, huge dorsal fins broke the surface—sharks had arrived. One-by-one a scream echoed across the still water as an Arawak was torn apart by several sharks. A Carib later commented that he saw a shark with a wad of snakes in its mouth and was still attacking the men.

One hour after first spotting the Arawak trading fleet,

there were but two still alive. The two young boy's eyes widened with terror as Ahameke approached.

Several of Ahameke's warriors had boarded the large Arawak canoes that had been refilled with the Arawak trading goods. The Caribs were already paddling the prize vessels toward the small island where their friends awaited their return. The two Arawak youths sat secured together with honeysuckle vine ropes and with terror in their young eyes watched Ahameke with apprehension. The two boys were certain that they were to be killed and eaten by the cannibals. Until this moment they had only heard the many stories told around evening campfires, but now knew that all they had heard was true.

When Ahameke removed a Spanish steel knife from its sheath, both boys grunted like pigs. Sweat ran freely as his blade approached one boy's throat. Dark eyes clamped tightly shut as though the youth could no longer keep them open. When the vine holding the gag was severed, he gasped for air. The second boy did likewise as his gag was removed.

As a warrior severed the vines securing their hands to the other's ankles, Ahameke leaned forward to speak to them. "Do not ever thank Yemaya for not bringing you to sleep in her house at the bottom of the water world." He leaned down until his face was so close that they could feel his breath. "Do you know who I am?" Both boys shook their heads to indicate that they did not. "I am Ahameke, cacique of all Carib warriors, and it is I, not Yemaya who has allowed you to live. Into one of your own canoes we have put coconuts and a knife that was carried by one of the men who wear shiny clothes. You will have plenty to drink and coconut jelly to eat as you paddle swiftly home and tell your people what you have seen today."

As soon as the two Arawak boys headed toward the horizon, the Caribs in their canoes and their friends in the Arawak prize canoes headed back toward their home on Martinique.

After they were home, Ahameke called a council. "When Baracoraima learns of our attack with snakes, which he taught us to do," he smiled viciously, "he will be furious. Now we will plan an attack on his island that the Arawak call Trinidad. Bameeta will have her warriors ready to join our fleet in one hand." He held up his right hand with all five digits spread.

When word of the Carib attack with snakes reached Baracoraima, he was as furious as he had ever been, and swore to one day soon rid the Caribbean Sea of the dreaded Carib cannibals, even if it meant aligning his people with the hated white invaders.

. . .

Atupi allowed the boys to talk amongst themselves for a few moments after a breakfast of cassava bread and cold sweet potatoes from last night's dinner, and then he approached the group. "I will now teach you the legend of how Yayjaba created the world." He paused to allow the boys to sit around the fire pit in a half circle facing him, and then began speaking.

"When Yayjaba created the world, he created first the spirit of water and the spirit of wind. Then Yayjaba created the large pond and in the middle he placed the land. Into the waters of the pond he placed the swimmers—those who breathed above the water and those who breathed under the water. Then Yayjaba saw that the land was beginning to slide down into the water, so he created the swimmers that would live on the bottom of the waters. There they would always remain and feed on the bottom, helping to hold the land steady to keep it from sliding further into the water.

Then Yayjaba opened the Great Cave and brought all of the two legged, four legged, winged, crawlers, and the tiny oriri insects. Each moved out onto the land and found a place for their home. Wind and water roamed over the land. Wind brought cool breeze in the heat of day, and water brought refreshing rain to the face of the land. But as they roamed, Yayjaba saw that more land was being lost into the water. The swimmers living on the bottom were holding as tight as they could, but they could not stop the land from falling into the water. It was then that Yayjaba created the one-legged ones. He said to them, 'you are my silent ones with no voice with which to speak, and you have been given but one leg, so that you can stand but can not move. But you are to do wondrous things—you will be the protectors of the land. Where I place you, you are to grab the land and hold it still. When Wind wanders the land, you must hold the land steady so that his breath does not blow the land into the water, and when Water wanders the land, you must hold the land steady so that his rain does not push the land into the water. All of you from the mightiest oak to the smallest flower, to the single blade of grass, are to hold tight to the land.

For doing this, the one-legged ones are to be given special gifts. You will amaze all others with your ability to live anywhere. You will find homes in the crevice of rocks, on the face of mountains, in burning sand, fertile land, arid land, in fresh water, and salt water. Some will be given stinging needles, and some will provide food for many. Some will seek your shade, while others find homes in your arms. Some will live but one cycle, but will have many children to continue your kind forever. Others will see more cycles than any other and will become the true ancient ones of the land. You will all be the beginning of the cycle of life and the continuation of all life cycles. When you fall to the land that you so faithfully held, you will become part of the land, and your children will take hold where you stood for so long and they will draw strength from you, thus you will continue forever.

All that has come out of The Cave and onto the land must show you great respect. They will know that you are the protectors of the land. When they lose that respect, and cast you down before your time, then the breath of Wind will blow that land and fill the air with dust. All who lacked respect for you will suffer greatly. Water will roam the land and to those who did not show you respect, he will give too much rain, and the land will be washed away. The waters will carry away those, and the others who showed no respect for you will get no rain until they dry up and are blown away by the breath of Wind. All who bring destruction to you will bring destruction upon themselves. You are my silent ones, and have but one leg and must forever stand in one place, but it is you who are the protectors of my land."

The old storyteller paused for several minutes allowing the boys to absorb the Legend of Creation, and to think about its meaning. Finally he spoke. "This is why we can take no one-legged one without first asking for permission. We must explain our need and approach with great respect and ask forgiveness with respect. To cast down a one-legged one before its time has come, and with no respect, is to bring about our own destruction." Atupi sat back and folded his thin old arms across his belly and watched the boys.

The five boys had remained silent as Atupi told them the legend, and remained silent. Each boy was thinking about his words, re-affirming something that Atupi had become certain of during the past few days. *This is a very exceptional group, which will yield great warriors, and perhaps a cacique.* "Remember that you must never remove anything that Yayjaba has placed on the land unless you first ask permission. Every single thing that he placed here has a purpose, and Yayjaba will help you if you treat all of the land with great respect."

9

~ Hurricane ~

Ahameke had moved half of his people to Dominica and joined forces with Caribs who had lived there for many years. He turned when he heard someone moving behind him. It was in the wee hours of morning and he was sitting alone at a small fire while contemplating the raid on Baracoraima. He was surprised to see his oldest medicine man staring down at him. Otamo had joined him in the move to Dominica, even though he was the oldest man in Ahameke's village; one hundred years old, by his own count, but Ahameke thought perhaps older. He was an old medicine man when Ahameke was a young warrior. "Hello old man, I am pleased to see you up and looking so well, because you have been ill."

The old man used his thin walking stick to ease himself down. When he was settled on the sand he turned to his cacique and said one word. "Yehebeti."

"Yes, old one." Ahameke turned to him, "Bad weather has been building since I came here to sit and think."

The old medicine man sat silently staring at the sky for several minutes, before speaking. "When darkness returns to the other side and shoves the sun from her sleep beneath the water, begin moving all of our canoes to the center of the island and tell the people to climb to the top of the mountain and to carry plenty food and water." He slowly struggled to his feet, and then looked down at Ahameke. "You will not have long to do this."

Ahameke watched as the old man limped slowly and painfully toward his hammock.

By noon, the men had tied carry-poles to the gunwale of twenty-two small dugouts and had already moved them a half-mile inland to an area where many coconut palms were planted years earlier, for the purpose of securing the dugout canoes when a storm was coming. The dugouts were left upright so they would fill with water and be heavy. Many thick vine ropes were crisscrossed over them, and then the entire male population returned to camp. A few young men had been left to tie stout poles across the gunwales of the remaining ten huge dugouts. These vessels were between forty and sixty feet long and almost four feet wide—and heavy. Poles were lashed to the gunwale every four feet, and protruded out on each side far enough that two men could stand at them side-by-side. With sixteen strong warriors on each side, the war canoes were dragged, one-by-one across the sand and along a worn trail created specifically for this purpose, and then secured to the outer area where the smaller dugouts were. Each of the huge dugouts was first filled with items not carried to the mountaintop, and then secured with vine hammocks before being turned upside down. By late afternoon, every one of the dugouts were thoroughly lashed to the nearly unmovable palms, as men and boys began filling their arms with bundles and headed toward the mountain, two miles away.

At midnight the wind was blowing very hard, and by morning harder than any of the old men had seen during the years they had lived on the island of Dominica. Winds of the hurricane pushed waves high onto the low lying land, but one mile up, on top of Mount Morne Diablatins, Ahameke's Carib people were safe. A multitude of deep lava craters surrounding Boiling Lake had been many years previously, thoroughly modified to accommodate all of the Caribs during hurricane season. As trees were ripped from the ground and giant waves thundered across the low land below, over one thousand women and children huddled as they prayed to Guabancex, their Goddess of storms and wind and water. Nearby, nearly half that many Carib warriors did the same. Many had survived hurricanes, and many had lost friends and relatives to them, but none had ever seen a storm such as the one threatening them now. All watched helplessly as whirling tornados bounced about inside the hurricane; competing with her by lifting huge boulders and trees into the air like toys before tossing them back—as though by a spoiled child having a temper tantrum.

The old people who had seen hurricanes knew that none had ever dropped their spinning black funnels into the craters. All prayed to Nana-Bukuru; not venturing so much as a peek above the rim.

When the eye arrived, many children who had never been through a hurricane, wanted to leave the crater to run and play in the sun. The older wives in their household had taught mothers, even the very young ones who had also never witnessed a hurricane, to forcefully prevent any of the children from leaving. When the backside of the hurricane arrived, with more power than its initial impact, everyone except the very smallest children at once understood the wisdom of their elders.

The thirty miles long by fifteen miles wide, island was stripped of much of the lush vegetation used by the Caribs as food and material for their daily use. Many palms were ripped from the sandy soil when hit by two hundred mile an hour winds.

Once the storm passed, both the small island and the Caribs immediately began re-establishing their dominance over Mother Nature and her fickle, unpredictable ways. The smaller palms near Ahameke's camp, which were only blown over, were propped up with short poles and the roots again covered with soil. Vines used for rope, lashings, hammocks, and many other things, which were killed by salt water, were gathered and stripped of leaves while they were still green and very pliable. Dozens of the young boys and girls began using them to make new hammocks, which would all be slept in that same night. Older boys and girls began cutting poles for new thatched houses, while others cut and stacked palmetto fronds to cover the frames, which the older men were already constructing.

All of their canoes had weathered the storm with no damage—testimonial to their ability to understand Mother Nature and cope with her changing moods.

One week after the hurricane passed, the Caribs' homesite was as it appeared prior to the hurricane's arrival. Clay pots sat on coals as a variety of seafood, plus small animals and rodents were added, along with a variety of root crops grown on raised areas of soil, reinforced with decaying vegetation and seaweed that had been washed by rain. The gardens were fertilized with water from large clay pots, into which all unused seafood items were tossed.

As life in the Carib village resumed, and the mess left behind by the hurricane was removed, Ahameke and his war caciques were in council planning the biggest raid ever on Baracoraima's Arawak village on the island of Trinidad, three-hundred miles south.

Trinidad is a large island, which lies just off the north coast of Venezuela, and was hit much harder by the hurricane than Dominica. Soon after brushing the Canary Islands she wandered around near the Mid Atlantic Ridge like an enraged bull elephant with nothing in sight to vent her anger on. Tiring of her isolation, she abruptly turned south and headed straight toward South America.

Dominica had received a direct hit, as did Martinique, but then she wandered east before turning south again to dance between St. Vincent and Barbados in the Tobago Basin, before continuing on with her wild spinning dance of destruction. Without a wide expanse of sea to dance in, she lingered over the coast of Venezuela, Trinidad, and Tobago—the tiny island a short distance north of Trinidad.

Winds over two hundred miles an hour raised havoc on the forty-miles-wide by sixty-miles-long island of Trinidad, whose elevation in the area where Baracoraima's village was established seldom exceeded two-hundred feet.

The huge cacique gathered his war chief's together and gave each their orders. "All but a few of the new canoes were destroyed when trees fell on them, so you must go to the big island to see how many are still sea worthy. If Ahameke learns that we have lost them he will soon attack us." Without hesitation, all thirteen men turned and began gathering supplies needed for a trip in their small dugout pirogues.

. . .

Captain Diego de Bazan fulfilled his mission in Africa, and with trepidation, scanned the darkening sky ahead as his fleet approached Venezuela.

Several weeks earlier, his superior officer, Admiral Juan Batista Topete Y Barca, had arrived with his entourage at the dock in Lisbon Portugal, on the morning of Captain Bazan's departure. The captain snapped to attention and smartly saluted. "Good morning, Admiral."

The Admiral ignored the saluting man and scanned the ships resting at anchor in the nearby bay. "I was under the impression that your sails would be full and heading toward Senegal by now to load the slaves." The obese Admiral turned back toward the captain; wine-filled veins pulsing near the surface of his swollen ever-reddening face.

"We leave on the noon tide, Admiral. Governor Don Carlos Greco has sent word that we were to await the arrival his coach."

The name of his immediate superior subdued the short Admiral's pompous air of distinguished infallibility. "Ah, yes! Of course, do not begin your departure until certain that you thoroughly understand his orders. Our settlements in Brazil and Venezuela need those slaves as soon as it is possible, but Governor Don Carlos Grecos' wishes come before all else."

The captain saluted again, but the admiral had already turned toward his coach. "Of course, Admiral Barca, I will...he lowered his hand as the Admiral's slave rushed to open the door. Moments later the coachman's whip struck the horse, and the vehicle lurched forward.

Before it was even out of sight, another coach, much less elaborately decorated, turned from the dusty main road and headed toward the dock area. The captain watched as it approached and he recognized it as Governor Greco's work vehicle; due in part because of the two huge black horses pulling it, and also the fact that it was so plain. The governor was a hands-on bureaucrat who spent many days among the people—getting things done...tasks that others talked about but seldom accomplished.

"Good day, Governor Greco." Captain Bazan sincerely liked the elderly man, and when the footman ran from the rear platform to open the door, the captain held out his hand to assist the governor as he stepped from the coach. "When are you going to retire and begin to enjoy the fruits of your many years laboring for our people?"

The thin little man clasped Captain Bazan's hand in both of his, and smiled. "When there are more men in our navy like you, and none or at least less like that bloated little oaf who just left."

"Does not appear to be much hope for you to retire soon, then." The captain's one raised eyebrow and a sly sarcastic smile brought a grin to the governor's face.

"Diego," the old man placed his hand on the captain's shoulder, "I do believe that if we had a dozen men in our navy like you and your father, God rest his immortal soul, we could kick all like Admiral Barca out." He paused a brief moment then grinned, "just imagine the money we would save on food and wine." When the captain only smiled but remained silent, the governor beckoned him to move to the wooden bench beneath a nearby shade tree.

Once seated, he looked around before leaning toward the captain, and speaking quietly in a conspiratorial voice. "General Alphonso d'Albuquerque is the man in charge of our African outpost in Senegal. You must trust no other person there, regardless what they might say to you. The general has been paying the local chief of all the tribes in that area to gather for us the information concerning the locations of gold mines. You will be receiving almost two thousand slaves to load aboard your vessels, but more importantly you will also load ten strongboxes filled with ore for our assayers to check. They are to be loaded upon your vessel and stored in your private cabin." He turned to the captain and spoke in an ominous tone. "If this ore is high in gold content it will be the salvation of the Spanish Crown. I trust no other man but you Diego, so guard the strongboxes carefully and let no one know what is in them." He motioned toward his driver, who was standing near the coach's door.

The man snapped his fingers loudly to summon the footman, a black African relocated to Lisbon many years earlier. The two men carried a wooden box to the governor.

The old man lifted the lid to reveal hundreds of small, gaudy, cheap jewelry items. "There will be ten of these placed aboard your vessel, Diego. The Africans treasure small baubles such as these far more than we treasure gold. These ten boxes will make the chief vastly wealthier than even our king." He smiled, and then motioned for his driver to prepare to leave. Governor Greco took Captain Bazan's hand and shook it; surprising him with the strength he had in his frail old hands, "God speed and good luck."

The day that Captain Diego de Bazan sighted land, he realized that his huge ship and the five smaller ones, which made up his fleet of slave transporters, were soon going to be hit with a hurricane. His navigator, Dom Enriquez, informed him that they were in the one hundred mile wide channel between Grenada and Trinidad, and approximately fifty miles from the coast of Venezuela.

The captain was a decisive leader who accepted the situations he encountered, and made the best of them. This was his third trip into the area to deliver slaves to work the mines on the mainland, or the plantations on the scattered islands of the Caribbean where many of the new Portuguese colonies had been established.

He turned to his ship's First Officer, Lieutenant Salvador Marquina. "Raise the flag to notify the fleet to follow me." The man issued the order and then stood with extreme apprehension as the captain conferred with the navigator; knowing they were in a very precarious situation.

"As I see it, we have very little choice, Lieutenant Marquina. We'll run through Dragon's Mouth Channel and into the Gulf of Paria. If we can make it through, we'll then find a reasonable lee to anchor behind Peninsula de Paria."

He turned to his navigator, a man who was obviously stressed. "Do you concur, Dom Enriquez?"

The small elderly man was silent a moment as he held his gray goatee and squinted his failing eyes while scanning the most current chart of the area: a prized document of that era. "Yes! I agree that we have no choice but to attempt the treacherous run through Dragon's Mouth, but that will be quite a feat, even for you, Diego." He stepped from the cabin to look aft at the five ships following. "For those men it will require a miracle."

Captain Diego de Bazan never moved from his station as the hours passed. He was at the elbow of the helmsman all the way through the narrow treacherous channel. When his anchors finally grabbed the bottom and brought his ship to a stop, the wind was at gale force and would soon be a full hurricane. The fifth of his smaller slavers made it through and anchored a mile west of his ship. Both were now protected somewhat behind a strip of elevated land hanging from the tip of Venezuela, somewhat resembling the tail of a debilitated opossum.

The other four vessels had captains on board with less experience, who also lacked the tenacity and endurance of their Fleet Captain who was trying to lead them to safety. Captain Diego de Bazan unabashedly opened the front of his trousers and urinated upon the deck where he stood. Four of the other five captains, at one time or another during the treacherous passage through Dragon's Mouth Channel, left the helmsman alone to judge for himself, and retired to their quarters for a glass of red Dão wine, or fresh clothes, or to urinate in their private toilet. It cost them their own lives—and the lives of most crewmembers aboard their vessels, and the lives of all of the slaves.

The first three ships to go down took all of their crew and over nine-hundred slaves, all chained below—to the bottom. The fourth ship was shoved onto the rocky shallows of Trinidad, where the storm tore her apart. Of the nineteen Portuguese sailors aboard, only the captain and five men were taught to swim as young boys and made it to shore, where they were captured by the Arawak who had been watching the foundering ship...their fate unknown to this day.

Below deck, almost three hundred black human beings huddled together; praying to a vast variety of gods. Their prayers were heard and answered. The superstructure was wrenched from the once stout hull, which made the vessel considerable lighter, and it bounced along the coral bottom toward shore.

The Africans saw that the timbers they were bound to, had begun tearing apart, and soon several men had freedom of movement. Still in chains, they combined their strength to begin a desperate effort to free the others. Once the bar running through their leg chains was removed, those who now only had chains on their feet could move around freely. Prying tools were hastily improvised to rip up the attachments holding the remaining long steel bars that tied the leg irons of the other slaves together. Rotten wood easily gave way to these men who were determined to live and help their fellow slaves join them. The steel bars were removed from the chains on their raw and bleeding legs and the Africans were at last able to stand and moved around.

When the remains of the hull began breaking apart, the slaves who could swim did so, and even hindered by the chains on their feet, they helped those who could not swim, hold to any object floating. Soon, almost three hundred Africans were wading onto the nearby shores of Trinidad—all still with chains on their ankles.

The Arawak watched, but did nothing until Baracoraima yelled loudly above the screaming wind. "Help the black people. They are enemies of the white men in shiny clothes."

All of the Africans were at first terrified to see several hundred small bronze men and women running toward them. When the Arawak began helping those injured during the ordeal on the ship as it started breaking apart, the Africans began silently thanking their many gods for sending these people to their aid.

Once the hurricane had passed, Baracoraima gathered to him several of the Maroons who had years earlier become members of his village. Among his entourage of blacks, there were a few who had recently come from Africa and had escaped from the Spanish mines in South America. They walked slowly through the Africans and continued speaking in the various dialects they were familiar with. At the end of the first day, Baracoraima was pleased that some of the Africans understood enough of what his Maroons were saying, that they could translate his wishes to the others.

"The men who build the big canoes are bad, and were sent here by Ghede and other gods of death. They want all who are not like them to be their slaves. The only way that we can prevent them from putting chains on all of us is to strike swiftly and kill them all." Baracoraima waited patiently as the Maroons translated his words while the Africans listened intently. Several young men gestured by picking up a stick and pulling it swiftly across their throat, that they would gladly join the Arawak in the killing of the men who had enslaved them.

Baracoraima listened as the Maroons explained that the Africans had been treated brutally; their women raped and sickly children tossed to sharks. Many years earlier, Akutatanna had arrived as a young African child among the Arawak. He studied the languages of the many Maroons who escaped the mines on the mainland of South America, and could converse with most. Baracoraima explained his plan and Akutatanna translated. "There are two large canoes near one of my villages with many of your black people on them, and messengers have come to tell me that the men in shiny clothes are bringing them out each day and throwing the sick ones to the sharks. I believe they will soon leave, and if they do we will never see your people again." He waited until he was certain they understood, and then continued. "We must strike them when they enjoy deep asleep, just before the sun returns. They have repaired much of the damage done by the storm, and after long hard days, my messengers say they sleep as soon as the sun goes back into the sea." He looked hard at the men nearest him, and could tell that they were ready to attack the Spaniards. "You are all still weak because these bad men did not feed you well, but we must attack soon if we are to free your people." When Akutatanna finished, many beat their chest first and then their belly, before yelling as if they were an organized chorus, one word repeated over and over...that Akutatanna said meant, kill them.

Baracoraima turned to his youngest wife, Dapalolee. "Find two of our best warriors, and tell them to have all remaining canoes that were not damaged by the storm brought to us near the water." Before the young girl even turned to leave, the old cacique turned to Akutatanna. "Tell the Africans to eat all they can, so they will be strong. We will be ready on the night after tomorrow before the sun returns from her rest in the sea." He waited until they understood, and then added with a huge grin. "The evil men have only two nights more to dream." The grin widened, "I hope they have pleasant dreams, because on the third night they will awaken to a nightmare."

. . .

Three hundred miles north, Ahameke sent word to his war chiefs that he wanted them all at his council fire. It was past midnight and all were sleeping, but they immediately rolled from their hammocks and headed toward their cacique's house. Once his wives, awakened from their sleep, had poured each a gourdful of cassava beer, Ahameke spoke. "Ogoun came to me tonight as I sat by my fire and pondered the damage this storm did to our villages. He put a vision in my head that was so vivid I thought he had taken me to the giant Arawak's villages on Trinidad. Everything was torn from the earth and tossed about as if a child was playing with their houses and sleeping places. Ogoun pointed at the scattered remains of the Arawak villages and spoke to me. He told me to attack the Arawak now, while the sea is calm and before they can rebuild their villages. He said we must go before they repair the big canoes that were damaged after rebuilding those that Raouti and Bameeta destroyed." Cacique Ahameke was so respected, that when he stood and instructed the chiefs to prepare to leave at daybreak, each finished his beer and headed to wake their warriors.

When the sun rose above the horizon, it fell upon the backs of five hundred Carib warriors—paddling south toward Trinidad. They stopped on Martinique and then again on St. Vincent, where their numbers increased.

. . .

As Baracoraima was organizing his Arawaks, and also the Africans, to strike the two lone surviving Spanish ships full of African slaves, another fleet of Spanish ships was also reorganizing. Two days sailing away, and directly east of Grenada, Admiral Ortiz Berenguer de Hidalgo gathered his fleet around his flagship.

A lifetime in the Spanish navy had taught him many things, foremost of which was to keep one eye always on the weather. Barely two hours from altering his course toward the island of Grenada and then on to Venezuela, he saw something in the darkening sky overhead that alerted him. He ordered a new course of due east, and as the hurricane that devastated the Windward Islands and Trinidad roared through with two-hundred mile per hour winds, his fleet is facing severe winds, and high seas, but they were nothing compared to the wind and water nightmare that Ahameke's fleet of Caribs, Baracoraima's Arawaks, and the remaining two Spanish slave vessels of Captain Diego de Bazan's small fleet began experiencing the following day.

. . .

Fate, and the uncanny intuition of the Spanish Admiral, had joined forces to create a situation that would alter the course of history, change the destiny of the Carib Indians, and seal the doom of the Arawaks Nation.

When the hurricane abated, the admiral set a new course. His fleet was now heading west toward Grenada, with plans to continue on to the Spanish settlement in Caracas.

Unknown to Baracoraima was the uncanny intuition and concern for the safety of the forty men on his vessel and half that many aboard his last remaining ship, was exhibited by Captain Diego de Bazan. The captain had been continuously searching the shoreline beyond his anchorage with his long brass telescope. Hour after hour as his men made repairs, his eye was on the telescope. He kept his thoughts to himself so as not to distract his men. *The savages are not showing themselves, but they are not good at keeping themselves concealed. I have never seen so many blacks among the savages during all of my trips to these desolate islands.* His diligence paid off late in the afternoon of the first day. *They are trying to keep us from seeing that they are amassing a large amount of those silly little boats they use, but it is becoming very obvious that they are planning to attack our two ships.*

Quietly and without haste, in case one of the natives also had a spyglass, he instructed Lieutenant Salvador Marquina to gather his gun crew and place extra ammunition near the swivelgun that sat atop the Captain's rear cabin, and the two that sat on each corner of the foredeck. "Do not open the gun doors, but load all six cannons on each side of your gundeck with grapeshot, and have them ready to fire if needed." Before the lieutenant could ask, he added, "We are going to be attacked by the savages who live on this island. In case one has stolen a glass and is watching our vessel, do not rush about while going on with your duties, and do not look their way."

Captain Bazan summoned his signalman, who a moment later was standing in front of him. "Tonight you must send a message to the captain of the Don Giovana, but it must be sent from an area where the natives on the shore cannot see it. Even though they could never understand what the flashes mean as you raise and lower the cover, we do not want to arouse their curiosity." He looked hard at the young man before he continued in a quieter voice. "I feel certain that we are going to be attacked, but I have said nothing to any of the crew except my First Officer. Decide where to send it from and assemble your equipment."

"Yessir," he said and turned around to head toward his work station.

The captain was ready for an attack on the first night, but nothing happened. The morning of the second day, he instructed his lieutenant to have the men stow their tools and begin checking the canvas and all ropes controlling the sails. "If we are not attacked tonight, then two hours before dawn, we will pull our anchor, begin raising full canvas, and sail straight back out the way we came in." When the lieutenant's red bushy eyebrows rose slightly, the captain said, "I timed our journey to this anchorage as we entered Dragon's Mouth, and noted the course, so I believe we will still be in safe water when the sun rises." The lieutenant saluted and began making all necessary preparations.

Shortly before nightfall Captain Bazan approached his lieutenant. "Have all crewmembers check to be certain their guns are loaded and ready to fire, before climbing into their bunks. Set a two-man watch, to be relieved every two hours through the night, and you and I will split the night in half, but tell all crewmen that we will arise three hours before the sun, to begin preparations to get under way. Caution them to be very quiet about it, because if the savages have not yet attacked, we do not want to warn them of our departure." He turned toward the shore and stared for a long period. "I will man the port swivelgun on the forecastle and you take charge of the one on the stern. Instruct gunnery sergeant Pintado Puron to listen for the anchor to be raised, and then have his men open the gundoors and winch the cannons into place." He stopped pacing and turned to his lieutenant, "Thirty minutes after the men are wakened I want this ship under sail, and as soon as humanly possible all canvas should be stretched tight." He paused to look at the sky;

rapidly becoming dark as the sun returned to the sea. He turned back to Lieutenant Marquina and smiled, "with a brisk morning wind filling them, I hope."

. . .

Bameeta, her brother Raouti, and their spies had brought valuable information back to Ahameke. He knew that he could not allow Baracoraima to complete the large canoes being built on Trinidad to replace those that his Carib warriors had burned.

Ahameke had now assembled a fleet of nineteen large war canoes, manned by almost seven hundred men. After he gathered new warriors and a few canoes on St. Vincent, he made a decision that changed the outcome of the sea battle; yet unknown to all who would participate. "We will go to the west side at Punta Penas, and then if we see no danger, head toward Trinidad. Raouti will go first with his smaller canoes, so that he can turn back and warn us if danger waits. I will follow with the main fleet, and Bameeta will remain in the rear with her three canoes to ensure that we are not attacked from behind."

As Captain Bazan was planning his cunning tragedy to outwit Baracoraima and his Arawak, Ahameke's fleet had already rounded Point Salinese on Grenada and was moving across a smooth sea toward Punta Penas at the tip of Venezuela's Peninsula de Paria—ten miles west of Trinidad. Raouti was nearby with his canoes, as was Bameeta with hers; both awaited orders.

A full night of paddling has brought Ahameke, Raouti and Bameeta to the shallow water near Punta Penas an hour before dawn. They gathered in the calm water in their war canoes, many of which were recently manned by Arawaks— to rest, eat, and discuss the planned attack.

Admiral Ortiz Berenguer de Hidalgo was blessed with fair wind and moderate seas as he moved into the channel between Grenada and Trinidad. Decreed by either chance or the gods, his large fleet has arrived in the area at the same time as Ahameke—and his several hundred warriors.

Unaware that assistance was nearby, Captain Bazan was moving cautiously in the pre-dawn darkness with full sails gathering wind. His course was leading his one remaining ship; sails stretched tight barely fifty meters astern, toward the northern exit from the Gulf of Paria—Dragon's Mouth Channel. He continuously searched the dark shoreline and the water between it and his two remaining ships through his long brass spyglass.

Baracoraima had not closed his eyes all night. Many stories were told about his uncanny ability to see things that others missed—even at night. He proved that the stories were true this night by awakening his war chiefs. "The big canoe is preparing to move." None had ever seen one of the large ships fill her sails and leave an anchorage before daylight, so they were skeptical. Baracoraima spoke quietly but with force; determined to rouse them into action. "The men who wear shiny clothes do not open the canoe's white wings unless it is time to move."

It required over an hour to get all sixteen of the Arawak canoes to the edge of the water and manned by the men assigned to them...almost one hundred of which were the recently rescued Africans—completely untrained, and most having never been on the water...except as chained slaves.

"The gun doors are open, sir, and all the men are ready." The captain responded with a nod but kept his eye on the glass's eye piece.

A moment later he said, "They're launching their canoes, so have sergeant Puron informed immediately."

By the time Baracoraima's fleet was finally organized and moving smoothly toward the two Portuguese ships, they were under sail and moving steadily ahead, but had not yet reached a speed that would allow them to pull away from the pursuing savages.

. . .

"Did you hear that?" Admiral Ortiz Berenguer de Hidalgo turned to Lieutenant Salvador Marquina.

"Yessir, definitely gunfire—cannons."

"Have the signalman use the lantern and instruct the fleet to reduce speed by half and stand by for orders." In the darkness, the message was relayed from ship to ship and soon all had reefed half of their sails and sent men to their battle stations.

"The men on the large canoe are shooting their big iron sticks at someone," Ahameke said to his brother-in-law, and second-in-command. "Perhaps it is the Arawak they are mad at? We will move ahead toward the tip of Punta Penas at a slower pace until the sun returns and we can see what it happening." He had the new order relayed to all canoes.

"I had not planned to run through Dragon's Mouth under full sails at high speed, but we must if we're to leave these savages behind. Raise all canvas and keep firing as they approach." Captain Bazan turned his glass astern, and spotting one of the canoes drawing closer, he went to the after deck and turned the deadly brass swivel gun toward it and waited. A few minutes later the roar of the brass weapon sent small steel balls flying down at the men, who were by then only a short distance behind. Half of then died or were wounded—one less canoe to worry about.

Gunnery sergeant Pintado Puron looked out the opened gun door and saw white flashes nearby. Knowing they were caused by the canoes, he ordered all cannons on both sides to be raised to the highest setting in the rear so they could be fired down at an enemy close alongside. He instructed his men to catch the grapeshot as they rolled out and to use a small powder load, then shove in chain, which was cut into half-meter lengths and kept nearby to be used for just such a situation as they now faced. "Leave the ramrod in the barrel," he yelled to remind them that the chain might fall out, otherwise. He looked out again and saw that there was now more than one canoe causing the white flashes. "Fire."

He spotted another white flash of water moving closer, but before he could order a cannon to fire at it he heard a blast from above. Lieutenant Salvador Marquina had spotted the canoe and fired the swivelgun. Sergeant Puron heard screams from the water and saw no more white splashing from the canoes. Their ship had finally acquired the speed necessary to move away from the natives.

Admiral Ortiz Berenguer de Hidalgo spotted the white sails a short time prior to the sun's arrival, causing the sky to lighten. When the sun finally peeked above the horizon, he could see the flag of his country streaming from the mainmast. Through his glass he also saw the canoes…some being left behind by the two ships, now that their sails were all up and full of wind; others turning back.

Ahameke had heard the gunfire and as soon as he spotted sails in Dragon's Mouth Channel and many more farther to the east, he quickly figured out what was taking place. He instructed his fleet with hand signals, to paddle hard and get behind the protruding isthmus then remain as low in the canoes as possible so they wouldn't be detected.

Captain Bazan had his signalman raise flags that requested the admiral and his fleet to follow him east to the open sea. One hour later they all reefed most of their canvas, and slowly reduced the headway to a knot an hour. A longboat was lowered and Captain Bazan was rowed to the admiral's boat.

Ahameke's mind was sorting out everything that he had witnessed. Once he had it all in place, he turned to his war chief. "We have already been to Baracoraima's village, and can easily locate it again. He does not know we are here, so we will move our fleet through the small channel between Trinidad and Tobago, then go ashore on the east side of

Trinidad."

Baracoraima was disgusted with his warriors for not using more caution to remain hidden from the eyes of the men in iron clothes, and for taking so long to get their canoes into the water, which allowed the enemy to escape. He said nothing now but decided that he would make a big issue of their poor performance later at a council meeting. He could see how exhausted and starving the Africans were, so they gathered all of those left ashore and then continued across the Gulf of Paria to Trinidad. By the time his fleet reached the western shore, Ahameke had already landed on Galera Point—the eastern shore.

. . .

Admiral Ortiz Berenguer de Hidalgo congratulated the captain on his ability to save his ship and one other from the hurricane, and also his cunning escape from a potentially disastrous situation. He suggested that the captain take his ship to Cuba and deliver the slaves to the authorities, and then have repairs made. "You can wait there and then join my fleet, and we will all return to Mother Spain."
    Captain Bazan thanked the admiral, and said he would meet in Cuba.
    After the captain returned to his ship, the admiral said to Captain Garcia Leonardo, "I had the pleasure of serving with his father. Both are very good men, and I suspect that he will be an admiral one day." He then turned to look toward Trinidad with a cruel expression, "let us now go load a few thousand slaves for delivery to our people in Caracas, then fill our bilges with gold and silver and then begin preparing for our trip to Cuba."

. . .

Ahameke had no intention of wasting time. He knew that Baracoraima would already be heading swiftly across the bay toward Trinidad. He was also very aware that the old Arawak and every warrior with him would be exhausted, while Ahameke's warriors would still be rested and ready to do battle with their lifelong enemy.

The memory of so many white wings and huge canoes remained a vision in Ahameke's mind as his men worked feverishly to remove all trace of their movement across the sandy beach. Before the admiral's fleet of seventeen ships had moved far from the spot that Captain Diego de Bazan began the long journey north toward Cuba, Ahameke was ready to begin moving his seven-hundred warriors straight toward Baracoraima's camp.

Baracoraima's warriors and also the Africans proved their worth by crossing the short distance in record time. After dragging their canoes into the jungle, all trace of their movement across the beach was removed, and the journey to their Arawak home village began.

Ahameke's Carib warriors had already reached the outer area of the enemy camp, and as planned, had separated into three groups. Raouti commanded one that circled around to the north, Bameeta and Gauban took another to the south, and Ahameke remained with the third. The few remaining Arawaks in the village were either very old or very young. All others had left with Baracoraima to attack the Spanish ship and rescue the slaves.

Completely unaware of the Caribs on his island, the giant Arawak led them into a trap. As they entered their village, the Caribs silently moved forward from the north and south, as Ahameke watched and waited on the east side of the village.

Confident that his son and daughter were in position, the command to charge forward was given by Ahameke. The sight of seven hundred screaming warriors charging them came as a complete surprise. For a brief deadly moment all of the Arawak warriors stood motionless and with shocked expressions...many died with that expression still frozen on their face.

Except for a few, the Africans were unarmed, save for a few sticks and hastily improvised clubs. They stood still as though they had already accepted their fate—death in a strange new land. When a huge black African began yelling in an African dialect that some understood, they told the others to drop any weapon they had. His words circulated quickly among the blacks, "he says they have come to rescue us from these people who will make slaves of us."

As Gauban and the other Maroons bashed in the heads of Arawak warriors who had rallied from their temporary stupor, they frantically herded their fellow Africans into an area where they would be safe.

Raouti and his men were dropping Arawaks so rapidly that soon they had to walk over their bodies to get to those who had gathered in the center of the village for an attempt to save their loved ones. Raouti moved past a warrior that appeared dead, but the Arawak suddenly stood and was about to brain the young Carib with his war club. One of the Africans that Raouti had rescued was standing behind the Arawak. The young African had just strangled another Arawak warrior with his garrote, and as the Arawak was about to swing his club he felt something slip over his head and tighten against his neck, while a knee was shoved into his back.

The commotion and the thrashing of the dying Arawak caused Raouti to turn briefly. He smiled when the African spoke loudly while still holding tightly to the garrote, "Me friend," he yelled in the Carib language.

Gauban turned away from the frightened Africans and saw a small Arawak poised with his war club raised, about to rush forward and kill Bameeta, who was battling three men, with her war club in one hand and her steel Spanish knife in the other. The huge African drew back his spear, and once launched by the muscles in his gigantic muscular arm, it flew straight to the mental target on the man's back.

Before the dead Arawak hit the ground, Gauban was on his way to Bameeta's side. His scream alerted her, but it startled another Arawak who was poised to strike Bameeta with his war club. The moment required for the Arawak to see where the scream came from, was all the time he was allowed to remain alive. Gauban's ironwood war club was transferred to his right hand as he lunged forward, and the Arawak's head almost exploded when it landed against his bronze forehead.

Ahameke spotted the giant Arawak at the same moment that Baracoraima saw him. Blood pumped through every vein and artery of the Arawak Cacique, but over twenty-four hours of continuous movement with no rest had taken a heavy toll on the old warrior's body. His wild swing brought the war club down toward his lifelong Carib enemy, but a rested Ahameke easily stepped to the side. The momentum of the swing carried Baracoraima forward and badly off balance, but Ahameke caught the old Arawak warrior before he hit the ground—on the blade of his sharp knife; taken from the hand of a dead Portuguese soldier in a battle many years earlier. While looking straight into the dark eyes of Baracoraima, the knife was pulled upwards, spilling his intestines upon the ground.

Baracoraima fell face down, but still struggled to rise and face his slayer. Resting on his hands and one knee, he felt Ahameke's bare foot press against his side and shove. The great Arawak leader lay prostrate at the feet of the Carib Cacique Ahameke. One hand still gripped the war club that he had entered many battles with, while the other tried in vain to place the intestines back into his deflated stomach.

Having never met the man standing above, he asked, "who are you?" in the Carib language.

Cold black eyes stared down as Ahameke replied, "The father of a young boy that you killed."

Baracoraima tried to recall which young Carib warrior it might be, but he had killed so many he soon gave up. As it began getting darker, the last thing he saw was Ahameke's war club coming toward his face.

Half an hour after entering the battle, every man, woman,

and child lay dead or dying. Still seeing visions of the big canoes with white wings, Ahameke yelled orders to Raouti and Bameeta. "Get the Africans and move swiftly to our canoes." His orders were never questioned, and within ten minutes everyone was moving fast toward their waiting seagoing dugouts.

• • •

Admiral Ortiz Berenguer de Hidalgo led his fleet through Dragon's Mouth and on to a safe anchorage inside the Gulf of Paria. Five days later he led them back out and set a new course for Caracas. "There was a very great battle not long before we arrived at the savage's village."

"Yes," answered the Captain, "do you suppose it could have been the blacks that Captain Bazan spoke of?"

The admiral pursed his thin colorless lips as a perplexed frown crossed his sharp chiseled face. He shook his head and spoke quietly, "perhaps, but whatever happened here cost the lives of many people." He stood on the deck of his ship with his hands behind, locked in an embrace as he looked across the terrain that his troops had just returned from. "We will forget about gathering a crop of slaves for the moment. There is no shortage of them in Africa, and" he turned and looked in the direction of Venezuela, "I suspect that there is also an unending supply nearby." His mind however was on something that he spotted earlier through his telescope as they entered Dragon's Mouth channel. At first he was certain that it was a group of canoes, but then dismissed the sighting as only trees blown into the sea by the hurricane. His mind now re-ran what he had seen, and it cause him to ponder, *could it have been those cannibals we have heard so much about?*

He turned to Captain Garcia Leonardo. "What?"

"I said it would save a great deal of time if we can get enough slaves in this area, and not have to go all the way to Africa."

The admiral's head bobbed up and down slowly as he pursed his lips, "yes, it certainly would."

• • •

Ahameke sat at his fire with Raouti, Bameeta, and Gauban. "With the Arawak village on Trinidad destroyed and their leader dead, it is now time for us to begin running the remaining Arawaks from these islands. We will begin with St. Lucia. Those who wish to join the Carib Nation will be welcomed; all others will be killed. Once we have relocated them to Carib villages, we will then attack Grenada."

Bameeta raised her calabash of cassava beer to her father and spoke with pride, "you will then have done exactly what you said you would, and these islands will belong to the Carib."

Had he known that the English and Spanish crowns were already renaming many of the islands that their explorers visited, and had plans to include all of them beneath their far-reaching political umbrella, perhaps Ahameke could have held them off a while longer, but inevitably the Carib Indians were doomed by the relentless thundering footfalls of modern mankind. They would eventually run as far north as the chain of Abaco Islands on the farthest northern end of the Bahamas, but to survive they were forced back to a small area on the Caribbean Island called Dominica. It is on this island that the last remnants of those proud people reside today.

• • • • •

Atupi sat silently staring into the fire on this last night atop the mountain. The five boys were instructed to add extra wood on the fire, and all knew why. "Tonight," Atupi said in a tone of voice that sounded ominous to each boy, "the fire must burn very hot." After several swift trips to the woodpile, during this last session that would end at dawn, the red-hot glowing coals were in each boy's mind.

They look like the eyes of a demon monster that has come to devour us, Ahanabi thought as he glanced back and forth between Atupi and the coals.

Uhubati was keeping his eyes away from Atupi. *I must not look at him or he will see the fear in my eyes.*

Bomatana could not keep his eyes from the glowing coals. *Vodun has come for one of us tonight,* his thoughts were similar to all of the other boys, and each had the same silent prayer, *Please Yayjaba, do not let it be me, because I want to become a great warrior.*

Podomani looked from Atupi down into the coals. His thoughts, more so than the others, was the reputation he would earn if it was he who was chosen by Atupi. *If I am chosen, I will be brave and take Atupi's hand and follow him. I will always be remembered as a great warrior.*

Atahana was often silent for very long periods while contemplating his teacher's words. Atupi knew that the young boy had great strength within. It was a very difficult choice that he was forced to make between Podomani and Atahana.

Atupi finally lifted his head and began a slow inspection of each of his pupils. His presence was so powerful that each boy lifted his head to stare back at the old warrior. He taught them never to break eye contact with any man—friend or foe once eyes had locked. He spent several minutes recalling each boy's strengths and flaws. One-by-one he slowly evaluated his young students, and would soon decide who would re-enter the village a month later as the greatest warrior among the five boys—if he passed the final test.

The coals settled lower and lower into the ten-foot-wide pit they sat around as Atupi evaluated the five boys, one last time. When his eyes locked on Ahanabi he thought, *he sees demons in everything, but he will learn to use them against his enemies.* He studied tiny Uhubati and thought, *he fears everything because he is so small, but I am small and fear nothing.* He stared intently into the little boy's eyes. *Yes! He will become a strong warrior.* He then concentrated on Bomatana. *He has not learned the spirits well and fears them all, but I will help him to understand that many are our friends who protect us.* Atupi observed Atahana a long moment. *His mind is powerful and he can see far into the future, and this will make him a great cacique, but his kindness will prevent him from acting swiftly in a time of crisis.*

When Atupi came to the last boy he looked far into Podomani's mind. He had decided early in the sessions that the powerfully built, self-confident boy was the strongest of his latest group. *This warrior will one day become a powerful cacique and many will follow him...just as these young warriors will now.* "Come around to me, Podomani, because it is you I have chosen." Atupi stood and looked to the east where a light would soon precede the arrival of a new sun. All of the boys' mouths fell open as they jumped to their feet. Podomani walked erect and confidently around to the old warrior and stood silently awaiting orders.

I must be strong, he thought as he stood in front of Atupi. *I will show no fear and will become a legend like Ahameke.* He was not yet thirteen-years-old but already the others were looking at him as their leader.

Atupi said quietly, "Take my hand and walk with me." Podomani took the leathery old hand in his and looked directly into the old warrior's eyes—never blinking. Atupi looked deeply into the young boy's eyes as he spoke. "I know that you have all heard small pieces of what you would endure here on the mountain with me, and the walk through fire was certainly one of them. Podomani, I will now tell you how you can follow me and never feel the fire and never have even a small blister. Close your eyes tightly and picture yourself walking through cool water toward Ahameke, who will present you to the entire tribe as a great Carib warrior." Atupi began humming a low but nearly hypnotizing chant as he took Podomani's hand and led him into the glowing coals. As they walked toward the other side, the young boy's mind was working for him.

Atupi has told us many times to be confident in our ability to overcome all pain. I will feel no pain as I follow this great warrior into my own destiny. Before they reached the other side of the fire pit, the boys were already looking at their young companion with awe and respect.

Atupi continued holding Podomani's hand as he spoke. "The final test will begin at dawn. Come! We must be at the water when the sun returns from her rest." The five youths had a difficult time keeping up with the old warrior as he moved swiftly down the mountain and through the jungle toward a small bay a mile from their village. The new young warriors had heard nothing about the final test, and followed the old Carib with great apprehension. Ancient law still kept even young lips sealed. *To speak of the final test to become a Carib warrior is punishable by death and the village elders will eat you.* No warrior had ever released the secret and only Atupi and the war council of elders knew...and of course the men who had survived it.

Atupi led the five boys to a hidden cache of five small dugout canoes. "In each is one paddle and one war club but nothing else." Atupi said simply, "Podomani." The boy remained rigid as he searched the darkness for his mentor's face. "As the gods watch, you are to be tested." He did not have to look at the other boys to see if they were listening— he knew they were. "It is a short time before the sun begins her journey once again from the ocean into the sky, so you will now choose which dugout you want. Go swiftly, fore when the sea releases her grip on the sun, and she slips once again into the sky, these four new warriors will also begin a final test. They will begin pursuit. Their task is to catch you and kill you, and then devour all but one arm with a hand that can be identified by the mark every Carib is given before going to the mountain."

He spoke again to the youth standing beside him. "Your task, Podomani, is to walk into our village when the moon has become round again, as it is tonight. Come, we begin.

When Atupi spoke again to Podomani, the sun was still below the horizon, but in a few minutes a small sliver of light would begin washing shadows from the five dugouts. "You may now choose your canoe, Podomani." He watched with admiration as the youth quickly inspected first the paddle, then the war club, and finally the hull of each canoe.

Without a word he pulled the small canoe he had chosen toward the beach, barely a few yards distant. Once on board, Podomani headed directly to where he knew the sun would first rise from the sea.

He paddled furiously toward the sun until he was beyond the vision of his pursuers.

Atupi watched as Podomani paddle straight out into the open Caribbean Sea and disappeared into the flashing liquid rays of the morning sun. The old warrior smiled slightly thinking, *he doesn't want even me to see which direction he takes. Good! He will surely one day be a great cacique.*

When the sea lost her grip on the sun, Atupi turned to the remaining four boys. "You may now choose your canoes and begin the final test."

When Podomani was certain that he was far enough at sea that his pursuers could not see him, he changed course toward the island of Martinique. It would be a fifty mile trip, and all knew that at this time it was an Arawak stronghold on the eastern end with a Spanish fort on the west end. From the moment he shoved the canoe into the surf, his mind was evaluating the possible directions that would be his best chance of survival. He finally settled on Martinique because two enemies of his people occupied it. *They will never come there, but I must wait far from land in this canoe until it is dark. When I have the canoe hidden in the jungle, then I must be very cautious and only search for food at night.*

• • •

Atupi and many others were sitting in the village beneath a half full moon, and thinking of Podomani and the four boys. A celebration was planned, but would not begin for two weeks when all five boys were once again with their friends in the village. If the four boys returned with a limb of Podomani, they would be hailed as warriors and would never again be spoken to as children. The fifth deceased young boy would be the guest of honor at the celebration, as many before him were, and be given the same treatment as a warrior who had died in battle.

One month after the trial at sea began, the moon was full as four boys entered their village for the first time since leaving with Atupi to climb the mountain. The entire population had been all night preparing a feast in their honor, and they now came running at the group of new warriors as the sun climbed the walls of the sky. They brought gifts of shell necklaces, decorated arm and leg bands, and a beaded headband with a variety of tiny shells. The village cacique approached them with his wives carrying five new ironwood war clubs. He handed each one of the elaborately carved wooden club. "You will each become a great Carib warrior and your name will be spoken around village fires forever." He looked hard at each new warrior before speaking again. "Did you bring a limb of Podomani?"

When a voice came from the top of a nearby coconut palm, everyone looked up. "They never got close enough to me to cut it off." Podomani came down from the top of the tall palm with the agility of a monkey. "If they had found me they would have died at the hands of the Arawak or the men who wear shiny clothes, fore I was in their midst the entire time I was gone."

• • •

On the day that the new warriors returned to their village, there was a celebration feast that not one Carib missed. Even the very young children were eager to hear about the adventure Podomani had while evading his four friends.

THE END

LEGEND INDEX (Carib)

ZEMI—Triangular carved stone—guardian deity of household

EMANJAH—TRINIDAD: river goddess—teacher of children

YAYJABA—Creator of the world

YEMAYA—Goddess of the deep sea

GHEDE—God of death

GUABANCEX—Goddess of storms-wind & water

GUANTUAVA—Guabancexs' messenger

LOA— Protector of humans

OLOKUM—Goddess of the ocean depths

BARON SAMEDI—God of magic and underworld

OGOUN—God of war

LEGBA—God of the Sun

ADAMISIL WEDO—Water Goddess

AIDA WEDO—Goddess of rainbows

DAMBALLA—Aida Wedos' husband (Fox God)

TUNPA—Tree God

NANA BURUKU—Earth Goddess

Epilogue

Those people who have heard of the courageous resistance by the Carib Indians, against the same invaders who ran them from their homeland in South America, often include the small Carib settlement on Dominica in their Caribbean vacation plans. Most leave knowing that they have spent time with a small group of descendants of those freedom fighters—who will soon be extinct. The peaceful Indians of South America, who always wanted only to be left alone by white invaders, had transformed themselves into the most feared of all Indians on planet earth. The tactics to survive that were used by the Carib has left them with an indelible stigma that will forever mark their race. It is that mark, left for the history of mankind, which will give this race of people immortality. Long after all other freedom fighters have drifted into the dusty, seldom-turned pages of history; many will still be able to recall stories about the Carib Indians.

RESEARCH SOURCE

THE TAINOS—Rise and Decline of the People Who Greeted Columbus—by Irving Rouse.

A Brief History of the Caribbean—by Jan Rogozinski.

The Internet.

Personal encounters with descendants of Carib and Arawak Indians.

Extensive travel throughout the Caribbean.

- **Dark Caribbean**...is based on a true story. Offshore lobstermen battle pirates for years, and eventually begin smuggling drugs. Airplanes, airboats, 150 mph pickemup trucks, gunfire, riding gators, wild men, wilder women—it's all in this one...and it's all true.
- **The McKannahs**...is a western adventure novel that begins in 17th century Ireland and moves to early 18th century America. 5 McKannah sons and 1 daughter spread out across this wild new country to build their life.
- **The McKannahs ~together again~** ... all four of the McKannah brothers come to Montana and stand with Jesse as he confronts men intent on wiping out his new family, the Flathead Indians. Their sister, Aleena...well, she..........
- **The Face Painter**...is a book of short stories for young readers from 8 to 88.
- **The Black Widowmaker**...was a beautiful black woman who made widows of many women, but after reading her story, you'll find yourself sympathizing with her.
- **Satan's Dark Angels**...is a collection of frightening dark stories that now accompanies The Black Widowmaker as 2 novellas in 1 book.
- **America**...is a book of western and other stories.
- **It's A Dog's Life**...the author's 15 year old, blind, Jack Russell(ish) terrier always wanted to write his autobiography. With help from Rick he finally finished it. All proceeds will go to homeless animal caregivers.
- **80 Stories**...is great for folks who don't like to face one long story in a novel. You'll find almost every genre in this one. Sad, chilling, funny, unbelievable, maddening, frightening, whacky, true, thought provoking, award winning and some, like a Father's Visit, that you will read over-and-over.
- **A Sacred Vow**...A memoir by Rick Magers.

- **Ladybug and the Dragon**...is the true story of Tampa, Florida native Katia Solomon. At 2 she was diagnosed with leukemia. Rather than write a story about her, as he was asked to do by a magazine editor, Rick decided to write a small book and have 6,000 copies printed, and send the Solomon family all of the money from signings throughout the south. Katia turned 12 on 26 January 2012 and remains in remission. Go to Rick's website www.grizzlybookz.net to learn how to order An updated copy signed by Katia herself.